Reviews from the original paperback, *A Hike for Mike:*

"... A GREAT DIARY of their trip, in which marathon runner Beth, a camping and hiking novice, encounters bears, lightning and freeze-dried food ... sheds light on a common condition affecting millions of Americans..."
—*Anne Stein, The Chicago Tribune*

"... His descriptions capture the magnificence of the varying vistas, the travails of the trail, and the camaraderie of hiking. Alt... candidly shares the joys and challenges of a long-distance trek and the positive discoveries that both he and his wife have made about each other. Reading about their journey is itself a reprieve from the frantic pace of everyday life. Indeed, Alt's conversational writing style makes one feel like a participant rather than an observer. Recommended for public libraries."
—*Jo-Anne Mary Benson, Library Journal*

"What happens when a marathon runner marries a hiker? In Jeff Alt's case, you get what NBC might dub Xtreme Honeymoon..."
—*Matt Bergantino, Cincinnati Magazine*

"... This book follows Alt and his wife Beth across the 218-mile John Muir Trail ... Encountering bears, lightning storms, rugged scenery, and fascinating people ... Non-hikers will enjoy the author's vivid descriptions of natural beauty and encounters in the wild ..."
—*LA Metro Book Review*

"... An amusing, stirring, true-life adventure ..."
—*Adventure Journey: The Extreme Vacationers Handbook*

"...They encountered hungry bears, dangerous lightning storms, tricky creek crossings and a sick hiker who needed emergency evacuation by helicopter; when their supplies ran low, Jeff and Beth even learned how to mooch for food and toilet paper..."
—*The Fresno Bee*

Library of Congress Cataloging-in-Publication Data on File

For inquiries about volume orders, please contact:

Beaufort Books
27 West 20th Street, Suite 1102
New York, NY 10011
sales@beaufortbooks.com

Published in the United States by Beaufort Books
www.beaufortbooks.com

Distributed by Midpoint Trade Books
www.midpointtrade.com

Printed in the United States of America

Interior design by Michael Short
Cover Design by Karrie Ross, updated by Michael Short

Four Boots
One Journey

*A Story of Survival, Awareness,
and Rejuvenation on the John Muir Trail*

Jeff Alt
author of the award-winning *A Walk For Sunshine*

BEAUFORT
BOOKS

To my amazing best friend and wife, Beth

Acknowledgments

F *our Boots One Journey/A Hike for Mike,* the journey and
the book, brought together a mix of family, friends,
and countless professionals, all of whom played a special
role making this book possible. I would like to extend my
sincere thanks to: Mary Richards-Beaumont, my editor, for
diligently and eloquently refining my manuscript into this
book. Mary provided necessary changes while maintaining
my style of telling a story. I'm especially grateful to my wife,
Beth, for picking up my slack around the house and with our
daughter as I focused on this project. I would like to thank
my entire family for providing counsel on this book. I really
heeded their advice. I would like to extend my gratitude and
admiration to my in-laws, for their courage and help, in spite
of the numbing loss of Mike, to make sure we got the story
right. I would like to thank my sister, Stephanie Pitts, for
her content suggestions. I would like to thank Kathy Morey

for sharing her Sierra Nevada expertise and advice. I would like to thank Bill Deitzer and Timothy Seaman for their constructive tips. I would like to thank Liz Osborn for her time and efforts in editing portions of this book. I would like to thank my webmaster, Georgia Sawhook, who played a key role in the success of our journey. I'm grateful to my publicist, Kate Bandos, for helping put together an effective media campaign. I would like to thank my publisher, Beaufort Books, and especially Eric Kampmann, Megan Trank, Michael Short and Felicia Minerva for releasing *Four Boots One Journey* into a paperback. I would like to thank all of the media, *The Chicago Tribune, The Cincinnati Enquirer, The Dayton Daily News, The Detroit Free Press,* and *The Reno Gazette Journal,* just to name a few, for helping to spread the word about our journey. I would like to thank all of the financial and gear sponsors for making this expedition a success. I am especially grateful to all the compassionate people who wrote letters and logged on to our website expressing their support for our journey. Lastly, I am grateful to John Muir for inspiring the preservation of some of the most beautiful landscape I have ever seen.

Disclaimer

This is a true account of the author's adventure along the John Muir Trail. Some of the names and details of individuals in this story were changed to protect their privacy. The John Muir Trail map has been modified and is not true to scale.

"Climb the mountains and get their good tidings. Nature's peace will flow into you as sunshine flows into trees. The winds will blow their freshness into you, and the storms their energy, while cares will drop off like autumn leaves."

—*John Muir, Our National Parks, 1901*

Table of Contents

The John Muir Trail, 218 Miles

California

San Francisco ○

BEGIN

Happy Isles, Yosemite
Elevation 4,035 ft

Mt. Whitney/Sequoia
Elevation 14,496 ft

END   Lone Pine

Los Angeles ○

San Diego ○

Introduction

The story you are about to read was originally published in paperback as *A Hike For Mike*. The new title, *Four Boots One Journey*, brings out the story line even more. On July 29, 2003, my wife Beth and I embarked on an expedition along the John Muir Trail, which treads the spine of the Sierra Nevada mountain range of California. For the better part of a month, we lived nomadically, relying on basic supplies and each other. This story is much more than a journal or travel memoir; it is a story of the commitment my wife and I made to each other, "for better or for worse, in sickness and in health." We made a unique commitment to each other when we joined hands in a life partnership—to hike over the hills and through the valleys of life together. Little did we know how real our metaphor would become.

Four Boots One Journey is filled with adventure, humor, and inspiration. I will explain the planning and preparation required for a high mountain expedition such as the John Muir Trail, and then take you on the trail with us. From the moment we set foot on the trail, you will walk alongside us as we encounter a menacing bear, lightning bolts, a mountain rescue, the constant threat of mountain lions, food shortages, fascinating characters, and altitude sickness. You will read about how we learned things about each other that we might otherwise have never discovered. When you remove yourself from the hustle and bustle, throw in a few intense situations, hunger, and a stunningly beautiful mountain backdrop, you gain an appreciation for each other's strengths and weaknesses that makes your relationship stronger.

I persuaded Beth to take this hike to help her work through the grief she experienced in the aftermath of her brother's death. We dedicated our hike to Beth's brother Mike, who tragically took his own life. Mike's family overwhelmingly agreed that his suicide was the result of untreated depression. We walked the trail not only as an adventure to get away from it all, but also as an awareness campaign for depression.

After learning that depression awareness could possibly save lives and compel those who might be suffering to seek treatment, I realized that there was something I could do. I am not an expert on depression, and I am by no means qualified to counsel a person who has lost a loved one. What I can do, however, is hike, and I am considered something of an expert on hiking for a cause. Several years ago, I walked the Appalachian Trail as a charity project. I thought we could turn our hike along the John Muir Trail into an awareness campaign for depression.

I had only known Beth's brother Mike for four years as his brother in-law. Beth had obviously known him her whole life, and even though they lived several states apart, Mike and Beth had remained close. She was hurting badly and trying to cope with his loss. John Muir, the namesake of the trail, understood the power of a wilderness experience to rejuvenate both body and mind. I hoped that hiking the John Muir trail as a tribute to Mike might help Beth to start healing from her hurt.

The support we had during our journey from family, friends, and countless strangers kept our spirits strong as we trekked along. I hope you enjoy *Four Boots One Journey.* Thank you!

Chapter 1
The Sunny Side

Yosemite National Park near Half Dome,
along the John Muir Trail
July 29, 2003

I had been married for nearly four years, and I was about to embark on my first long-distance backpacking adventure with my wife, Beth. We had planned to trek across the spine of the Sierra Nevada Mountains in California on the John Muir Trail. It was no easy feat convincing Beth—a woman raised with the belief that vacation meant flush toilets, sleeping in a bed, soaking up the rays on a beach, and eating out—to throw on a pack and live in the woods for the better part of a month. This was our first visit to California. After months of planning, we had crammed our backpacks full of gear, food, and supplies. After flying into Los Angeles from our home in Cincinnati, Ohio, we had visited a few much-talked-about California wineries before arriving by shuttle bus in Yosemite National Park. Beth and I had positioned ourselves in Yosemite Valley, near Happy Isles, the northern terminus of the John Muir Trail, and had planned to walk the trail's entire 221-mile length.

The John Muir Trail, or the JMT, is named after one of the world's most noted naturalists. You have to do something on a grand scale to have an entire trail named after you, and Muir's advocacy and appreciation for the wild earned him the distinction of being named the father of our national parks. One of his favorite areas was the present-day Yosemite National Park. Muir once hosted President Theodore Roosevelt on a camping trip in the park, which seemed to convince the president to save the Sierra from development—not long after Roosevelt camped out with Muir, Yosemite was protected as a national park.

I had walked the Appalachian Trail five years earlier and had been itching to take another long-distance hike. Although the JMT is only a tenth of the Appalachian Trail, it is considered a world-class hiking path. The trail stretches from its northern terminus in Yosemite Valley to its southern terminus high atop Mount Whitney, the highest peak in the contiguous United States. It passes through three national parks, two national forests, and a string of mountain peaks with rocky surfaces as jagged as saw blades and as high as 14,491 feet. By comparison, the Appalachian Mountains on the East Coast top out at 6,643 feet. The John Muir Trail is speckled with glacial lakes and wilderness that are untouched by roads and most other civilized amenities. It's hard to find trails unblemished by roads in today's world. It joins with the Pacific Crest Trail for much of its length, and it is the most rugged and arguably some of the prettiest terrain of the entire West Coast.

We were scheduled, according to our wilderness permit, to begin our expedition of the John Muir Trail on Tuesday,

July 29, 2003. Our trek was expected to last two to three weeks. We spent a last night of civilized comfort in Yosemite National Park, in a canvas tent cabin built on a wooden platform. Our abode was anonymous among 628 identical bungalows in Curry Village, a cozy little camping area with no vacancies. People were everywhere. A massive, rustic wooden commissary located in the center of the tent village provided showers, a buffet-style cafeteria, an outfitter, a convenience store, a food stand, and even an outdoor bar with a featured beer—Sierra Nevada Pale Ale, of course. Adjacent to the main building stood an old log structure that served as a sitting room, game room, and even a U.S. post office. It was the most disparate combination of modern amenities and rugged outdoors I had ever seen.

Along the parking lot next to the commissary, tourists were gathered around trunk-size steel containers. They were stuffing food, snacks, and toiletries into these bear-proof chests under strict direction from the park service. Warnings were posted everywhere advising against consuming food in the tent cabins or keeping any scented toiletries.

Stunning views beckoned from every direction. With the commissary to our backs, our left field of vision was filled with the famous Yosemite Falls cascading off an immense sheer cliff, taller than most city skyscrapers. To our right was Half Dome, a mountain sliced in half during the Ice Age which has become the park's symbol. Beth and I wandered out to the field just in time to see the sunset. A woman standing nearby looked dazed and dreamy and exclaimed, "This is what the Garden of Eden must have been like."

John Muir, a Scottish immigrant, came to America, fell in love with Yosemite and its surrounding wildlands, and advocated for its preservation. We were smack-dab in the middle of the valley where Muir had spent quite a bit of time. While most early settlers to California were busy tending farms, searching for gold, or building cities, Muir was taking in the natural beauty of the wildlands. He had the foresight to realize the land was in jeopardy of succumbing to the loggers' axes and the developers' shovels. He had in fact lived for some time in the valley not far from where we now stood. None of the coffee-table books could replicate the raw beauty we were witnessing. It really brought home Muir's passion about preserving the park.

We weren't the only ones awed by the view. Each year, millions of tourists flock to the park Muir loved. According to Yosemite National Park records, in 2002 alone, more than 3 million people visited the park by foot, car, and horseback. As we watched the sunset, the mountains were changing colors almost as if a slide projector was clicking to the next frame every few seconds. Various shades of orange, red, purple, and blue emerged and faded almost as quickly as they appeared, with a darkening sky creeping over the peaks. The tops looked glowing hot, a phenomenon known as alpenglow.

Later that night, Beth and I tucked ourselves into bed with the false sense of security one feels after zipping shut the door of a thin-walled tent. As we were fading off to sleep, terrified shrieks and the loud, metallic banging of pots and pans shattered the night. Someone had apparently ignored the warnings of keeping food out of the tents and now was trying to scare away a bear using the recommended procedure of making lots of noise and hurling objects toward the animal. We both lay awake, excited about the adventure we would begin the next morning and thankful the bear was bothering someone else.

My wife's courage ran too deep for a bear to scare her. Beth was embarking on a journey completely outside of her comfort zone for a cause greater than herself. This was more than an adventurous vacation. We were walking with a purpose.

Chapter 2
My Hiking Spouse

Cincinnati, Ohio
August 21, 1999

F ive years ago, I walked the 2,160-mile Appalachian Trail, an adventure chronicled in my first book, *A Walk For Sunshine*. In this book I mention my pursuit of a relationship with my friend Beth. I attended graduate school with Beth, and from the first day I met her, I knew she was the one. She was the first woman who stopped me in my tracks and made me go to great extremes to appear to be a gentleman—the perfect gentleman for her.

Beth was an athletic, petite, brunette with a soft, warm personality. Being friends with her was easy. The more I got to know her, the more time I wanted to spend with her, but all through graduate school, Beth wasn't ready to establish a relationship beyond friendship with me. After all, she was seven years younger than I, and she lived in a flat midwestern suburb of Chicago, which she knew did not appeal to me at all. But we both were very fond of each other, so much so that all of our close friends were always telling us that we should be more than friends. Some even speculated that we were secretly more than friends.

Beth met me on my Appalachian Trail journey for a weekend. I thought for sure that she had deeper feelings for me. Unfortunately, we departed that weekend still just friends. It wasn't until recently that she confessed, "Jeff, you really stunk." Well, I was showering only once a week. I was wearing synthetic clothing, which has an awful tendency to retain the body odors we normally try to eliminate in order to maintain relationships. I wasn't wearing deodorant so that I wouldn't attract bugs, and I had been living among the animals for more than 800 miles since I had left Georgia. My patchy, shady-looking beard made me look more like a fugitive on the run than an attractive, eligible bachelor. After that weekend, I continued walking toward Maine, another 1,300 miles from where I left Beth in Virginia. This gave me time to get used to the possibility that she and I might never be more than friends. After all, we had known each other for almost three years, and she still hadn't fallen for me.

What I didn't know was that while I was walking in the woods, Beth had come to the realization that I was the one for her. According to legend, several of Beth's family members—after hearing Beth talk about me—would say to her, "It sounds like you really like Jeff as more than just a friend." *The Oprah Winfrey Show* caught Beth's attention one day with an episode on relationships. It left her with this advice: "Look under your nose for that special person."

The problem with this tip was that I was right under Beth's nose, and I stunk. Eventually, Beth got around to developing a relationship with me. After returning from my journey, the

Sunshine hosted a dinner party and slide show in my honor. I had dedicated my journey to my brother, a Sunshine resident, and had raised money for the home, which is a haven for developmentally disabled youngsters. Beth was one of a few hundred in attendance. We spent that entire weekend together, and at one point I asked her, "If you aren't married in five years, would you marry me?" She said, "Yes."

This was a long-shot question, and she gave me a long-shot answer. She had told me of another friend of hers that she had a similar pact with. I think the fact that I was now showered, shaven, and separated from my smelly hiking gear had a lot to do with her response, especially with Oprah's olfactory advice. I was determined to follow through on our pact. Our relationship developed quickly because we already were great friends and we knew each other very well. We were engaged four months later, and we married in August 1999.

We stepped from the church on our wedding day wearing backpacks bearing "Just Married" signs. I had to spend quite some time convincing Beth that she would still look beautiful in her white wedding gown even wearing a backpack. I also figured that this would send a clear message to everyone that Beth had now become a hiking outdoorswoman. This didn't exactly turn out to be true. Beth is very athletic, having run three marathons, so physical fitness wasn't an issue. Also, she had joined me on dozens of day hikes, so enjoying the great outdoors wasn't an issue. The issue was her appreciation for domestic amenities. Beth would avoid staying overnight in the woods at all costs.

Hiking had become a lifestyle for me, so we made a premarital pact that if Beth would do an overnight hike with me, I would run a marathon with her. This resulted in an insane honeymoon that included several long runs, including one 18-mile cataclysm in preparation for the Chicago Marathon. In turn, Beth donned a backpack with supplies for "a, one, *uno*" night in the woods—hardly a fair deal considering the determined training regimen to run a marathon. On our honeymoon, Beth turned what was meant to be a two-night backpacking excursion into a one-night affair. She flew down the trail so fast that we covered double the miles we planned for one day, ending up back at our car a day earlier than expected. Beth knew that if we finished early, she would be able to stay in a hotel. In spite of her hasty hiking experience, I filled my end of the deal by running the 1999 Chicago Marathon with Beth.

I figured Beth would think back and romanticize our overnight adventure in the woods—like I tend to do after every hike—and crave more overnight hikes. But after our adventurous honeymoon, Beth declined all my offers to come along on extended hiking trips. She liked her hot showers and warm bed. To her credit, she has a disorder in which her fingers and toes turn purple and become excruciatingly painful in even moderately cold temperatures.

In spite of our opposing preferences for vacations, we were happily married. Our marital journey had embarked from the trailhead full stride. Then, like a hike in rugged country, we descended into a valley of unanticipated tragedy, which forever changed Beth's attitude toward hiking.

Chapter 3
Mike

Toledo, Ohio
September 2002

On a sunny, warm September weekend, Beth and I were in Toledo, Ohio, three hours north of our home in Cincinnati. We were celebrating the fifth annual Walk With Sunshine for the Sunshine Children's Home. My 1998 benefit walk on the Appalachian Trail inspired this annual 5k walk, which raises funds for disabled people. Every year since my hike, I have helped organize the event, including giving a motivational speech to kick off the walk. On Saturday, the day of the walk, we were blessed with sunny weather, a bluegrass band, the largest walker participation since the walk's inception, and animals to pet from Sunshine's animal barn, which the walk would benefit. In my speech, I reminisced about my original walk, pulling examples of perseverance and the spirit of Sunshine. Beth and I spent that Saturday evening with my father and stepmother—both Toledo residents—at a relaxing cookout before driving back to Cincinnati. On Sunday morning, Beth and I got up and went for a morning run in my favorite Toledo park, Wild Wood Preserve. The weather had changed from sunny to dark and rainy, foreshadowing the events that were about to unfold.

When we returned from our soggy run, my stepmom said, "Beth, call your mom." We soon found out that Beth's brother Mike was missing. Beth is the youngest of four siblings and the only girl in her family. Her three brothers lived in the Chicago area, where they grew up. Beth was closest in age to Mike, and they were very close emotionally. Beth's family is so close that Beth was the maid of honor in Mike's wedding, and her two brothers were the best men.

Beth's brothers and dad had gathered at Mike's house after a frantic call from Mike's wife, and they had organized a search party. Beth's mom was at home in case Mike showed up. When Beth hung the phone up after talking with her mom, she had tears running down her cheeks. This was, she explained to me, not like Mike. I suggested that Mike might have gone to a friend's house and that everything would be fine. We decided to get on the road back to Cincinnati; there was no reason to sit around and wait for news. We were 30 miles south of Toledo when our cell phone rang. It was her brother Brian. As Beth listened to Brian, her demeanor changed dramatically from calm and hopeful to upset. Tears streamed down her cheeks. "No!" she cried. "No, no, why, why, why?" Beth was distraught. She blurted out, "Mike's dead."

I was shocked. Mike had killed himself. My stomach was knotted. All I wanted to do was hug my wife, but I couldn't let go of the steering wheel. I got off at the next exit and pulled into a truck stop. Beth was a mess. We remained in the far corner of the parking lot for quite some time. Slowly, we made our way back to Cincinnati—making calls to friends and family, who helped us make flight arrangements to Chicago. Shortly after returning home, we left for Chicago to be with Beth's family.

Beth and her entire family were grief-stricken and grasping for answers that would never come. It seemed as if life had stopped. There was a son without a father, a stepdaughter without a stepfather, a wife without a husband, parents without a son, siblings without a brother, nieces and nephews without an uncle, countless friends without a pal, and everyone without answers. This isn't supposed to happen. Mike's family had their lives turned upside down overnight.

All of us kept asking ourselves over and over, *Did I miss something?* When someone dies from an accident, in battle, or from cancer, loved ones often get an answer to the "why" of it all. Those deaths aren't self-inflicted. Most families know that their loved ones tried to survive by taking precautions, whatever solace that offers. But when someone takes his or her own life, the questions raised are countless.

Beth began attending support groups for people who have lost loved ones to suicide. She met regularly with a grief counselor, and she dived into every book about depression, suicide, and grieving she could get her hands on. At first, I had been angry that Beth's brother would do this. Naively, most of us think of suicide as a cop-out. I thought Mike had to have known he would put his family into a spiral of grief and misery. The grief counseling Beth attended explained that Mike was suffering inside, and that he thought suicide was his only remedy. Mike obviously wasn't thinking clearly. He was depressed, and he didn't follow through with the proper medical treatment.

As Beth learned, she began to give me a crash course in psychological studies of depression. She would toss out signs, symptoms, and treatment strategies, always leading with, "Jeff, did you know that...?" I had lost an uncle to suicide, and I began to take interest. I thumbed through some of the information Beth had collected and found that it is widely agreed that depression is the primary cause of suicide. This was the first time that I realized that my uncle most likely suffered from depression. I considered myself reasonably educated—I had a master's degree, after all—but I had never correlated depression with suicide until then. If I was clueless to this little piece of information, then I was sure a good percentage of the population hadn't connected depression and suicide, either.

Beth had spoken with Mike on several occasions about fatigue, and he told her that he had taken anti-depressant medication but had stopped on his own accord, without a physician's recommendation. Mike had assured Beth everything was all right. According to the National Institute of Mental Health, depression is a clinical condition treatable through medication, therapy, or both. The medications that doctors prescribe for clinical depression alter chemicals in the brain. A medical consultation is required for decreasing dosage or switching medication. Most of those who follow their doctors' directions recover from depression. If Mike's depression had been properly treated, he probably still would be alive.

Prevention is the key. A recent story on ABC News quoted a psychologist who had tracked 500 people who had been prevented from jumping to their deaths from the Golden Gate Bridge. The doctor said almost all of them were still alive years later, except for a few who had died from natural causes.

The National Institute of Mental Health reports that 31,000 people commit suicide every year. That's similar in numbers to those who die from prostate or breast cancer. With all the research and treatments available for cancer, you would think that similar efforts were in place to educate the public about the symptoms and treatment for depression and the prevention of suicide. Some excellent resources and organizations are in place, but more needs to be done. This condition can't remain the elephant in the room. How can we tolerate the staggering number of deaths to this illness?

Knowing that depression can lead to suicide and that depression can be treated, then shouldn't this be considered an epidemic with immediate measures put in place? Why not turn this situation into a success story for modern medicine? It seemed like the logical step. The tough part about depression is that it's not tangible. You don't get a CT scan or MRI to pinpoint the problem, like with other illnesses. You can't remove some tissue or go through chemo. But you can go to your doctor. You can take the prescribed medication or do the therapy, and chances for survival are well in your favor.

I wanted my wife to be happy again, but I felt helpless. I hated seeing Beth so sad. It was my duty to protect her, but how could I shelter her from this?

Chapter 4
We Need a Hike

Cincinnati, Ohio
February 2003

Whenever I have been in a tough spot with a major decision or personal crisis, I have headed for the hills. For me, just looking up at a mountain range sets off a soothing feeling inside. Not long after embarking on a forested mountain journey, I begin to feel the burden and pressures fall away. Giving up the domestic comforts of a hot shower, television, and refrigerated beverages in exchange for a clear mind is worth it. I don't mind getting grit under my fingernails and a layer of dirt on my body, or washing off with a cold mountain stream water and sleeping on the ground. For me, it's all worth the opportunity to put all life's daily distractions aside and fully concentrate on my inner thoughts.

I have always thought that the mountains are God's thinking room. Cultures from around the globe have associated God with the mountains—the Chinese, Egyptians, and Greeks, to name a few—with good reason. Mountains have an intimidating immortal awe about them as they loom up to touch the sky. Climbing in the mountains exposes one to many of God's natural beauties and natural dangers. When I get far enough from civilization—physically and mentally—my acuity of all God's creations around me increases and makes me realize my place in the world. It is with this peace that I realize however difficult and horrible the circumstance is, God is there to help me work through it. He has a plan, even when I don't. Sometimes I emerge from the trail with answers to my dilemmas. Sometimes I leave the woods with more questions than I had going in. But I always feel refreshed and glad to be alive to enjoy this great world. I would have loved to take Mike on a hike.

In the late 1980s, I faced my own mortality. I had been trained as a U.S. Army combat engineer. I was at the top of my game, young and healthy. I had a college fund and my whole life ahead of me. Then, one day, I was involved in a severe accident. My arm was trapped underneath a sliding truck, which had flipped onto its side. It snapped my left humerus like a pretzel. The bone pushed through my bicep, completely out of my arm and up against my chest. It severed most of the nerves branching into my arm and missed my main motor nerve by a hair. The truck continued to skid, yanking the rest of my body along for about 30 yards before finally coming to a stop.

I was pinned in a prone position looking up at the sky. Emergency professionals arrived and ran all around, assessing the situation and carefully working to remove the truck from my arm without causing further damage. I could smell blood soaking my clothes and the ground all around me as I lay helpless. At the hospital, I overheard the doctors discussing my condition. Shortly before I was put under anesthesia for surgery, I heard the word "amputation." I was surprised to wake up with my arm still intact and wrapped in very thick gauze. One of the best bone surgeons available happened to be on call that day, and he saved my arm. He set my humerus back in place with the help of a permanent six-inch-long titanium plate fastened down with screws. On an X-ray, my arm resembled an Erector Set creation. I was one lucky guy. It could have been my head under that truck. God had granted me a second chance at life.

The Army honorably discharged me, sticking to its policy of no pins, no plates, and no screws. That was okay, though—I was alive. My arm was cemented in an L-shaped cast for six months. When the cast finally came off, it was with the help of a physical therapist and encouragement from friends that I slowly began exercising. It quickly became a daily ritual. My future seemed in disarray at the time, but my approach to life had radically changed.

I had decided that I was going to live each day as if it were my last, now acutely aware each day actually could be my last. What would I do if this were my last day on Earth? I wanted to hike. As a teenager, I had backpacked in the Great Smoky Mountains, so I decided to return there. During that excursion, a feeling of confidence warmed my entire body and mind. I felt alive again. I could climb mountains. The pine and flower fragrances of the fresh mountain air coursed through my body. Walking in the woods had become my own self-prescribed medicine. I climbed the ridge of life once again.

+ + +

For me, a survivor is someone who moves on, overcomes, adapts, learns from his or her experiences, and shares with others how to avoid getting caught in similar situations. I had been planning to walk the John Muir Trail in the Sierra Nevada. My last major expedition had been a fund-raiser, but I hadn't planned to put together another walk for a cause until Mike's death. Why not dedicate my upcoming walk to depression awareness? It could help people understand the symptoms and treatment of depression. I shared my idea with Beth. I explained that she could be my support team— although I really wanted her to hike with me—and we could create a national awareness campaign, which would give Beth an opportunity to work through her loss by doing something positive and to help prevent someone else from following the same course as Mike. Beth liked the idea, but she still hadn't signed on with any interest of hiking with me.

In February 2003, five months before my planned departure on the John Muir Trail, we took a trip to visit a hiking buddy I had come to know from my Appalachian Trail adventure. After completing the Appalachian Trail, he went on to walk the Pacific Crest Trail. The Pacific Crest Trail joins with the John Muir Trail for most of its length. My friend shared some of his photos of the Sierra Nevada. The snow-covered granite peaks were cut with sharp angles, towering high above the trees and pushing into soothing blue sky. The stunning photographs must have been enough to convince Beth. On the drive home, she casually announced, "Jeff, I want to walk the John Muir Trail with you."

Beth had broken through one of the stages of the grieving process. She was ready to leave the mindset of being a victim of her brother's death and become a survivor, taking charge and working through her family's tragic loss in a positive way.

Beth has never served in the military. But with a soldier's courage, she was facing the depression demons that took her brother's life. She decided that the symptoms and treatment for depression should become household knowledge. Katie Couric had a live, nationally televised colonoscopy performed on herself after losing her husband to colon cancer. She worked to help overcome the stigma associated with the invasive colonoscopy procedure. Beth and I were going to try to decrease the stigma associated with getting treatment for depression and decrease the number of suicides.

There have been many recent improvements in educating the public about depression, but many remain unaware that this is a treatable illness. *The Chicago Tribune* would soon quote Beth in a nationally syndicated article as saying, "We are going to be very vocal [about depression awareness]."

Beth, like the rest of her family, was experiencing a tremendously hollowing loss, but she had made a decision that would help her survive this tragedy and help others. Beth was about to embark on a trek that would help her climb out of her dark valley and continue on the journey of life.

Chapter 5
Finished Basements

The Outfitter, Cincinnati, Ohio
Spring 2003

It had been four years since our honeymoon hike. Many of my trail friends had spent their entire married lives trying to prod their spouses into such an adventure, and here we were actually going to do it. In spite of the circumstances that convinced Beth to hike, I was determined to make this a romantic experience; even though we were walking for a cause, we needed to enjoy the journey along the way.

For Beth, this hike seemed the perfect remedy for her to do something positive in honor of her brother and the treatment of the disease that led to his death. She says that Mike would have wanted us to enjoy the adventure together and that he would have been proud of her for taking on such a challenge. From my brief brother-in-law relationship with Mike, I learned of his quick wit and enormous sense of humor. Mike could quote lines from the '90s sitcom *Seinfeld* off the top of his head. On several occasions, Mike and I threw around book ideas, all with a comical nature to them. I remember one of his book ideas was to write about the funny situations parents encounter while raising children—such as whether it was up to dads to teach boys the unwritten rule of which urinal stall to use in the men's john.

Humor helps me in difficult times. It's a relief to find something to laugh about in tough or grim situations—it's even healing. Perhaps Mike's humor was his way of coping with his secret battle with depression.

Beth and I agreed (or should I say I convinced Beth) that this hike would be a great opportunity for our relationship. For the better part of a month, we would sleep in close quarters—un-showered, of course—and would be together 24 hours a day, a plan which in many cases has either built or ended relationships. On the other hand, we would experience one of the most spectacular trails in the world together. Not only would we be together on the trail, but we also would spend the next several months preparing, planning, and training.

This was no ordinary hike. We were about to trek across some of the most beautiful and rugged mountain terrain in the world. Most who have hiked in the West will define the Sierra as one of the sunniest, mildest (in the summer) high-elevation climates in the world. Many who have walked the Pacific Crest Trail confirm the John Muir Trail to be one of the most beautiful but toughest sections of the entire length of the Pacific Crest Trail, which runs from Mexico to western Canada. Most JMT'ers complete their treks in 15 to 30 days. However, in many ways, preparing for our adventure was just as tedious as preparing for a five-month Appalachian Trail or Pacific Crest Trail trek. An adventure such as this requires logistical planning, physical training, and assembly of the right gear, in addition to the extra tasks we took on with our depression-awareness campaign.

The first order of business was to get a backcountry permit. Due to heavy use, the national parks and national forest service regulate the number of hikers in the backcountry. In 2002, Yosemite National Park issued 49,924 overnight wilderness permits; of those, 945 were JMT thru-hikers. Annually, more than 19,000 permits were issued to summit Mount Whitney, the southern terminus of the JMT. Four months before our proposed start date, I contacted a Yosemite backcountry ranger and reserved two of the last remaining permits for the date we planned to start in Yosemite at Happy Isles, the northern terminus of the JMT. The reservation only cost a few dollars, and it assured Beth and me a date to start.

Backcountry trails are frequently rerouted to prevent erosion, and logistical re-supply locations and businesses that cater to hikers change ownership or go out of business. That makes having the latest guidebook essential. *The Guide To The John Muir Trail* by Thomas Winnett and Kathy Morey became an indispensable book for planning our trip. It was the most current guidebook we found for the JMT. The guidebook proved invaluable with its mileage distances, elevation profiles, suggested mail drops for supplies, and maps. I like maps that I can unfold and place on my lap like a napkin. It puts me into an expeditionary trance as I ponder thoughts of how far I've walked, where will I stop for the night, what's the name of that mountain vista I just snapped 20 pictures of, where exactly was it that I lost all my food to a bear, etc. Initially, we ordered forest service maps for the entire trail based on information I found on a website about planning a JMT trek. When we received the maps however, I realized how impractical they would be. The maps were made of paper, which a slight rainfall would convert to nothing more than an unreadable spit wad. Also, they unfolded to the size of a bedspread, requiring five people to utilize—one to hold each corner and the fifth to navigate. Even if you had five people, a gust of wind could tear the giant maps to shreds. We ditched these and found a map pack by Tom Harrison Maps to suit our needs. This is a pack of 13 notebook-paper-size plastic waterproof maps. They were colorfully designed, easy to hold, and would prove their quality by surviving numerous coffee spills, downpours, and river crossings.

We dubbed our adventure "Hike For Mike" in honor of Beth's brother. A co-worker from the school where I taught responded to an ad I posted on the district bulletin board searching for a web designer. My colleague put me in contact with her mother-in-law, who had been dabbling with HTML and web design out of her home. She had three websites online that have had half a million hits combined, underscoring her web prowess and creativity. We were her first paying customers. Being the wife of a pastor and mother of six, she was very compassionate about Beth's brother's death. We met several times, providing her with text files and pictures. By March 2003 our website, www.hikeformike.com was online. Our webmaster didn't realize at first that she had become our command and control. We didn't, either. As it turned out, she would be our only link to our families and others following our journey as she updated our website.

Our website became the main tool of our awareness campaign. We had a page about depression signs and symptoms, a page about Mike, a page about the John Muir Trail, a page about Beth and me, a page where we would post our trail journals, a photo gallery, a sponsor page, and a media page. Our goal was to reach as many people as we could on a tight budget. With the consultative help from my publicist, Beth and I sent press releases to the proper media contacts who would find our awareness adventure interesting.

Within a few months, we had articles appearing all over the country. *The Chicago Tribune, Detroit Free Press, Dayton Daily News, Cincinnati Enquirer, Reno Gazette Journal,* and dozens of other newspapers from California to New York told our story. *The Chicago Tribune* story about "Hike For Mike" cited a study from the Journal of the American Medical Association that discussed the need for better diagnostic approaches and the high instance of depression. E-mails began pouring in from all over with tragic stories of suicide deaths, concerns regarding depression, and inspiring stories of those successfully battling this silent illness. We responded to every one of them.

Our journey would not only help get the word out about the signs, symptoms, and treatment for depression, it also would promote the important role our national parks play in our physical and mental well-being. It's no secret that exercise helps you feel better about yourself. It's well documented that in addition to the physical benefits you gain from regular exercise, you also decrease your stress and anxiety levels. Hiking is a rigorous sport, which, if done on a regular basis, definitely has a physical and mental impact. "The medical and academic communities agree that hiking in the great outdoors is a natural way to increase your body's antidepressant chemicals in your brain" (Hiking Against Depression, *Reno Gazette Journal*, 7/23/2003). These are the same chemicals that anti-depressant medications stimulate as one of the treatment protocols of depression. That said, hiking or exercise is not a replacement to seeing your physician if you think you have depression. Every person has different needs. There are excellent medications a physician may prescribe to treat depression, with exercise as a supplement.

Someone experiencing depression might be turned off by monetary requests on our website during a time of despair, so we didn't feel our awareness campaign should serve the purpose of raising money. This raised the issue of how would we pay for our awareness campaign. We didn't have the funds to pay for all this ourselves. We had to come up with money for web design, monthly web server fees to keep our site online, publicity costs for a media campaign, a publicist, postage, thousands of copies, travel money, and hundreds of dollars in phone expenses. Friends, family, and countless others came to our assistance by sponsoring our awareness campaign with monetary contributions.

We arranged sponsorship with GMPCS satellite communications to provide us with a satellite phone to communicate real-time trail journals as we moved along the trail. In addition, several gear suppliers donated quality gear, which cut down on our out-of-pocket expenses and led to a successful expedition.

Beth and I began training for the trek four months before our departure. Because we maintain a regular workout regimen, it wasn't too hard to add a few extra training exercises specific to our adventure. We both continued our running schedule three to four days a week for at least 30 minutes, along with weight training two times weekly. As part of our enhanced hiking training, we walked on an inclined tread-

mill with hand weights to simulate walking poles twice weekly, with packs on our backs. We simulated crossing dangerous
streams by fording across our living room into the dining
room to get used to crossing as a team. Beth enrolled in a
spinning class, which is an organized stationary bike workout
that focuses on leg strengthening and cardiovascular training.

Our dining room and kitchen began to resemble a hiking
supply center. I dusted off my dehydrator, which hadn't seen
heavy use since my Appalachian Trail adventure, and we began drying vegetables and meats. Several boxes lined the walls
of our dining room floor and were heaped with supplies. One
box contained supplies for the first half of our journey, which
we would fit into our packs as our departure date approached.
Another box contained the supplies we would ship off to an
outpost along the trail as our only re-supply.

We made several trips to the grocery store and local out-
fitters, carefully selecting food and gear. Our dinners would
consist mostly of freeze-dried meals and a few of my favorite
grocery store foods that work well with hiking, such as macaroni and cheese, ramen noodles, and vegetarian beans. Our
breakfasts would be a mixture of toaster pastries, granola
bars, energy bars, and coffee. Our lunches would include
peanut butter, pita bread, assorted cheeses, summer sausage,
beef jerky, and foil pouches of tuna and chicken. We collected all assortments of energy bars, athletic gel packs, candy
bars, and Gatorade. Toilet paper was rationed and sealed in
plastic bags. My first-aid kit was inventoried and replenished,
adding bags of cotton swabs, vitamins, and ibuprofen. Extra batteries for our flashlights and camera were assembled
into bags. Our packs, boots, hiking clothing, stove, tent, and
other odds and ends filled our study. I set up the tent in the

backyard to make sure we had all the poles and stakes. We cooked dinner on the hiking stove several times to get used to its features. Two months before our anticipated departure, we took a three-day shakedown hike to the Great Smoky Mountains National Park with all our gear to make any final adjustments before heading out to the John Muir Trail.

Beth and I were almost ready for our adventure. We had some of the best outdoor products in the industry sponsoring our expedition. Beth had a Marmot rain suit; we had lightweight Lowa, Gor-Tex lined boots—the best pair of boots I have ever worn. We had the new MSR featherweight backpacking stove, Cascade Designs Therm-a-Rest mattress pads, Exerstrider hiking poles, Slumberjack and Marmot down-filled sleeping bags, Princeton Tec lightweight headlamp flashlights, a Kelty tent, and a Shakespeare fishing pole. All of the sponsored equipment proved essential to our California expedition.

I was used to whittling my gear down to the bare essentials, but Beth was getting a crash course. On my suggestion, she grudgingly chucked her lipstick and makeup, replacing them with sunscreen and lip balm. Over time, she slowly got used to living without sedentary luxuries: her coffee would lack the flavored cream she ritualistically pours in each morning. She would have to leave behind her shampoo and soap in exchange for wet wipes, and would ditch her terrycloth towels in favor of air-drying in the cold mountain air.

We had fully prepared for our expedition, but hadn't addressed one controversial hiking garment—underwear. Underwear to long-distance hikers is like cream and sugar to coffee drinkers—some folks can't live without it, and some folks prefer to go without. For me, underwear meant friction, which resulted in painful sores in the creases of my legs. But my wife's requirements needed to be taken into consideration, so we paid a visit to the local outfitter. We didn't want to chance it by ordering something as personal as underwear over the Internet.

I had never shopped for woman's underwear, let alone in an outfitter shop. Traditional tighty whities don't work in the woods—cotton is the last fabric you should wear in the great outdoors because it holds moisture to your body, causing rashes and even a drop in body temperature, which can cause hypothermia. Beth and I picked through the selection of women's underwear hanging on the racks. I didn't know what we were looking for, and Beth apparently wasn't satisfied with what she had seen so far.

A young man with dreadlocks was standing behind the nearby checkout counter, and he asked if he could help.

"Yeah, we're trying to find some hiking underwear for my wife, but she can't find what she's looking for," I stated as we approached the counter. "Hey, Beth, can you tell the guy what you need?"

Trying to be as helpful as he could, the clerk pulled out an order catalog as Beth explained her underwear demands—blushing, of course, since she had never ordered underwear from a man. The young man, also blushing, thumbed through a leading-brand outdoor underwear catalog as he began to learn more about my wife's underwear requirements than I had learned in more than four years of marriage.

In the meantime, I struck up a manly underwear conversation with another outfitter employee.

"Do you hike in underwear?" I asked.

"Oh, yeah, always," the employee responded. "Why, do you?"

"Nope."

"So you walk around the great outdoors with an unfinished basement," he said.

"Yep," I replied.

As I explained my painful hiking underwear experiences, he walked over to the men's section and tossed a rolled-up pair of name-brand boxer briefs into my chest.

"These are the best. You shouldn't have any friction issues."

I decided to give him the benefit of the doubt and added them to the pile of supplies Beth and I were accumulating on the counter. We left the outfitter that day with "finished basements," which actually turned out to work very well. As I wrote this, I learned that this specific outfitter went out of business. So if you're ever browsing in an underwear store and a male sales clerk approaches and asks you if you would like to finish your basement, trust his advice.

Beth's family wanted to be a part of our campaign. Our project helped pull her family together and gave them something positive to do while they healed from their loss. Beth's brother Paul had worked with Mike for ten years at the Chicago Board of Trade, the world's largest futures exchange. Paul was grieving the loss of a brother, but he had lost a co-worker as well. Paul and several of Mike's co-workers arranged a "Hike For Mike" casual day at the Chicago Board of Trade. Any floor trader wearing a "Hike For Mike" T-shirt could break from the traditional dress code and wear jeans on the trade floor on Friday, July 29, the day Beth and I were set to start the John Muir Trail.

A week before Beth and I departed on our expedition, Beth's parents, brothers, associates of Mike's and Paul's, Beth, and I stood behind tables stacked high with "Hike For Mike" T-shirts. We all were located strategically at the main arteries of the board, right in the middle of thousands of employees entering and exiting the trade floor. By the day's end, we had sold all 800 T-shirts and had legal pads filled with names backordering nearly 100 more. This was a huge outpouring of support. All proceeds—nearly $5,000 after costs—went to the Suicide Prevention Action Network.

Beth and I had agreed to keep fund-raising away from our "Hike For Mike" website awareness campaign. The T-shirt event worked perfectly and was a positive way to get the average Joe to buy a shirt and then log onto our website for more information. As Beth's brother Brian put it, "You will have 800 walking billboards of www.hikeformike.com." Brian arranged a wholesale deal on T-shirts through a family friend who knew Mike. The shirts were gray, made of high-quality preshrunk fabric with a three-color design on the front. It showed a picture of the mountains, and in bold yellow lettering, "Hike For Mike" spanned the top of the shirt with "The John Muir Trail" along the bottom of the mountain picture. The back of the shirt listed our sponsors, along with our website. Because the T-shirts were cotton, Beth and I had two synthetic hiking T-shirts made with a similar logo that we would wear on the trek.

On July 29, Beth and I departed by plane from Cincinnati to L.A. to begin our journey. While we were en route, 850 floor traders and staff donned "Hike For Mike" shirts and jeans on the trade floor to support our campaign. We wore similar shirts on board a 747 heading for California. This was a huge send-off as we began our adventure. Thousands had already logged onto our website, and thousands more would eventually log on as well, surfing all the pages including the depression awareness facts page.

After landing in L.A., we rented a car, drove up the Pacific coast, stopped at a winery or two, cut inland toward Yosemite, dropped our car in a small town near the park, and boarded a park shuttle bus to the northern terminus of the John Muir Trail.

Chapter 6
Here We Go!

Happy Isles, Yosemite National Park,
211 miles from Mount Whitney
July 29, 2003

The morning after arriving in Yosemite National Park, Beth and I awoke refreshed from a night's rest, despite our tent cabin neighbors' noisy bear encounter. Our tent cabin was furnished with a full-size bed. The temperature had dropped during the night, and we actually needed the wool blanket to keep warm. This was the last night we would spend in a bed for quite some time. The sun was peeking over the mountain. It was 60 degrees. We pulled ball caps over our matted hair, slipped into our hiking pants, and our "Hike For Mike" T-shirts, strapped on our sandals, and marched to the Curry Village commissary for the all-you-can-eat breakfast buffet.

After breakfast, Beth and I walked through an outfitter shop adjacent to the restaurant, browsing the gear as a last check to make sure we had all the essentials. We returned to pack up our belongings. We spread out our hiking items on the bed with one final check to make sure we had everything and to see if we could eliminate any unnecessary items. We packaged the road maps, the California car tour guidebook, and assorted toiletries we wouldn't need until the end of the trail. I addressed the package to the post office in Lone Pine, where we planned to spend a few days after completing our trek. We knew from a brief walking tour of Curry Village the day before that a post office was located next door to the wilderness permit office, where we would obtain our back-country permit that morning.

We marched down to the parking lot to retrieve our bags of food from the steel bear locker I had secured them in the night before. Beth and I then stood at the shuttle stop in front of the commissary. When the bus arrived, we stumbled aboard with our packs on our backs, carrying our hiking poles and a few bags of supplies that eventually would be crammed into our packs. We stepped off the shuttle near the Yosemite Wilderness Center.

We dropped our packs outside the center, leaned them against the wall, and walked inside. A smiling young man with beach-ruffled hair and a confident gleam in his eye greeted us from behind the counter, impressing us instantly as the guy we should talk to about our hiking plans. Behind him were black plastic canisters stacked against the wall in a pyramid that almost reached the ceiling. This ranger had walked the entire Pacific Crest Trail the previous year, so he knew the local backcountry. As he prepared our permit, he reviewed all of the rules of the backcountry and persuaded us to rent two of the food canisters stacked behind him—each a hard plastic cylinder the circumference of a brake drum with a bulge in the middle. They looked like mini beer kegs, and they weighed 2.7 pounds each. Each canister was fitted with a lid that had a recessed turn latch with a nickel-wide divot to lock down by using a coin or other sharp object. These canisters supposedly were bear-proof, but I was skeptical. I had read stories of how California black bears had heisted food from hikers after each hiker skillfully counterbalanced his food from trees by rope at least 10 feet off the ground, a procedure that is supposed to prevent bears from stealing food. The park service had photographs of car doors and trunks that bears had popped open with the same ease as a human cracking open a soda can. You had to admire and respect the bears' intelligence. I figured it was only a matter of time until they learned to file down their claws so they could turn the latches on the bear canisters without requiring the coins that we humans needed. Beth and I had squeezed nine days of food—enough to get us to our halfway re-supply point—into these containers and carefully fitted them inside our packs with all our other equipment smashed in around the canisters. I couldn't help but feel like a Sherpa carrying the bears' food bounty as I hoisted the loaded pack on my back.

We were all set to embark on the trail when I realized I had forgotten to ask the ranger about the wildfires. I had noticed a sign posted in the park that casually mentioned five contained fires in the park. Tourists milled about in a carefree way as if such fires were business as usual, but I wanted to be sure we would be safe. We had driven through a wildfire on our way up the coast to Yosemite. The fire engulfed the road, bottlenecking traffic down to one lane as dozens of firefighters battled the blaze. The native motorists acted as if this was all in a day's commute. They sipped their coffees and chatted on their cell phones as the oncoming cars zipped by with embers bouncing off their hoods, windshields, and roofs. Apparently, fires raging at least 30 feet above the ground aren't enough to cause alarm in California. Back home, schools would be canceled and every news station would be feeding live coverage of the inferno.

Most of my hiking has been in the Appalachians, which has its own fires. But I have never walked through a forest with five controlled fires. My brother Todd is a fireman and explained that fires are set purposely—and contained—to regenerate soil. Other times, they are used to eliminate underbrush as preventive measure so wildfires started by lightning or human negligence don't burn out of control. Todd acknowledged that sometimes contained fires burn out of control when Mother Nature jumps into the mix, like when a fire gets so big it actually creates its own wind and can travel quickly up forested mountains. Even trained firefighters sometimes get caught helplessly in wildfires with nothing more than foil blankets to wrap in like baked potatoes for protection. Beth and I dropped our packs off our backs, and I stepped back inside to ask the ranger a few more questions.

"Excuse me, sir, how will we be notified on the trail if a fire gets dangerously close?" I asked.

"We'll find you," the ranger assured. "And don't worry, they are all contained."

With all of Mother Nature's possibilities in such an arid climate—wind and lightning especially—I just wanted to hear some sort of rational explanation of what options we would have if a fire encroached on the John Muir Trail. The ranger assured us that officials would estimate how far along the trail we were and send an emergency crew for us. With the ranger's explanations, I felt somewhat reassured.

Beth and I slung on our packs and wobbled over to the post office to mail our package. We then stood along the road at the bus stop to catch the next shuttle to Happy Isles trailhead. Moments later, the shuttle arrived and we were soon dropped off at Happy Isles. With packs on our backs, hiking poles in our hands, and a wilderness permit in our pocket, we began our walk.

The trail was as wide as a farmer's lane. It was beaten down from the millions of tourists with whom John Muir Trail hikers share the footpath on the short trip to Half Dome. We followed the trail on a meandering walk along the Merced River and were shaded mostly by pines as we began our ascent out of Yosemite Valley. We were walking heel to toe with a sizeable herd of day hikers on their way to Half Dome. Among the day hikers were parents exposing their children to the wonders of the world and honeymooners adding an adventurous flair to their romantic getaways. There was an audible and visible international presence. We were walking with pep in our step that belied the anxiety of setting out on our adventure, but we were relieved to finally be on the trail and leave our domestic worries behind.

A few hundred yards from the trailhead, Beth and I came to a card-table-sized sign bolted to a post taller than my wife, listing the mileage to all the points of interest along the trail: Vernal Falls .8, Half Dome 8.2, along with nine other shorter destinations of less than 30 miles. At the bottom of the sign, Mount Whitney was listed dramatically at 211 miles, as if it was saying, "Come on, I dare you." Beth and I stopped and asked a passing tourist to snap a photo of us. We stood for the shot, my finger pointing at the 211-mile mark. As we smiled for our photo, a tourist passing by noticed our ambitions and offered his opinion in British dialect: "You'll never bloody make it." I wanted to catch up to the man and give him an earful of my hiking resume, but I calmed down and dismissed his comment, realizing he surely must have based his judgment of our success on his own capabilities. He seemed to be getting quite an earful from his wife for being so rude, anyway. Later, he offered us a thumbs-up and wished us the best as he rested along the trail, out of breath with streams of sweat running down his cheeks after only a half mile of relatively easy uphill. His wife was standing nearby, monitoring his comments.

We finally had begun our latest challenge. But I thought back to 1999, when Beth and I ran the Chicago Marathon together shortly after exchanging wedding vows. Mike, along with his wife and kids, stood at mile marker 8 holding a sign up that read: "Go Beth and Jeff." We were so excited to see them among the thousands of spectators lining the course that we stopped running, exchanged hugs and chatted as thousands of runners zipped by. They were such a happy family. I can still vividly remember Mike smiling so proudly holding his newborn son as he stood with his wife and step-daughter. They seemed like the all-American family. Mike was so supportive of his sister that he skipped Sunday church services and brought his family down to the marathon to cheer us on. How could a guy who loved his family so much, a guy who would be there in a New York minute to help a friend or loved one anytime, any place, end his life?

The trail continued upward, passing over a wide bridge below Vernal Falls. A domestic bathroom was nearby, and Beth decided to use it—she wasn't sure she would see another bathroom for a few weeks. We continued our ascent for several miles. Soon, we could hear a distant white-noise sound as we glimpsed Nevada Falls, a massive cascading waterfall alongside a stubby, treeless mountain peak. The water shot off the cliff in a stream and plummeted down the five-story granite rock wall before dropping from view into a pine forest canopy. A short while later, we emerged from the tree line into an open area above the waterfall. A bridge led us over the falls. Dozens of tourists speckled the treeless area. Some perched on rocks; others watched children frolick in the mountain stream that fed the waterfall. Beth and I dropped our packs and pulled out a stick of summer sausage, crackers, and a block of cheese for lunch. We sat eating lunch on an un-shaded rock slab, the sun baking us as the temperature neared 90 degrees. But masses of dark rain clouds were rolling in, so we didn't stay long. We chugged some water, saddled our packs, and moved along. We were finally on the trail. We were really doing this!

Chapter 7
Bear Courage

Yosemite National Park along
the John Muir Trail, near Half Dome
July 29, 2003

A few hundred yards from our lunch spot, we were once again immersed in shade that provided some relief from the intense midday heat. We trudged slowly out of Yosemite Valley and skirted Half Dome, famously photographed by Ansel Adams. Although we were expecting typical July blue skies, rain had threatened all day. We were somewhere around 7,300 feet above sea level in Yosemite National Park.

Almost every expedition I have undertaken has involved a bear encounter and this expedition was no exception. Movement off in the brush caught our attention as we rounded a bend in the trail. A rather well fed bear appeared and hoofed slowly towards us. It stuck its nose in the air, sniffing and looking at us. It was obvious it knew we were coming before we encountered it. It had cinnamon-colored fur with lighter patches, and we wondered for a moment if it was a grizzly. But we had been told that the last grizzly bear in the Sierras was shot in the 1920s, and the California black bear had been slowly filling the void ever since.

"What should we do?" Beth almost shrieked as the bear wandered toward us. I suppressed the surge of panic shooting through my brain and calmly conjured a reasonable answer: "Just walk slowly, and keep your distance." We managed to creep past safely, and Beth even snapped a few pictures.

During my five-month expedition on the Appalachian Trail in 1998, I never worried about black bears. They primarily eat plants and insects, and they turn to meat only when desperate. Although they have grown accustomed to human food, they are not typically above humans in the food chain like their carnivorous grizzly cousins, which prefer a meat diet that yes, at times, includes humans. My casual attitude about walking among black bears changed in May 2000, when an experienced female hiker out for a day hike in Smoky Mountain National Park was attacked and eaten by two black bears. The bears didn't touch the food in her backpack, which leads me to suspect that they may have traveled up the food chain. That was the first reported fatality by a black bear in a national park, although there have been black bear fatalities elsewhere. According to the California Department of Fish and Game, no black bear fatalities have ever been reported in California. But there have been numerous bear attacks. I didn't want to scare Beth with unwarranted fear of the animals, so other than assuring her that no hikers had been killed by black bears—in California—I kept the rest of the statistics to myself until after the hike.

Beth and I sighed with relief when the bear decided to leave us alone, sluggishly waddling off into the woods. We walked on slowly as we regained our stried, our pounding hearts slowly decreasing to normal levels. Not even half a mile from our first bear encounter, we ran into another. I picked up a few rocks to throw if it became necessary. Further up the trail, a young boy rounded the bend toward us. The bear stood on all fours between the boy and us and turned to look back at the boy. As soon as the boy saw the bear, he ran and clambered up onto a car-sized boulder on the side of the trail. The bear's instincts to chase kicked in as he quickly lumbered over to the rock and circled it several times. The boy huddled in the center of the rock, speechless with a frightened look on his face as he watched the bear's every move. The bear stood up on its hind legs and began slapping the rock with its front claws, which made an intimidating clacking sound. The boy had a knapsack on his back that probably was filled with snacks, and the bear might have been hoping the boy would share. The young boy looked frightened and helpless as he stood up on the rock.

"Where's my dad? Someone get my dad!" the boy shouted.

I threw rocks at the bear and began yelling. Luckily, the bear dropped back down onto all fours and looked over at Beth before slowly jogging off into the forest. Even though the bear probably only was after the boy's food, the boy feared for his life, and the one person the boy wanted was his dad—the symbolic pillar of courage, strength, and bravery who surely would be able to defeat 300-pound bears whenever necessary. Apparently, the boy had trekked ahead of his father on the way down the mountain from Half Dome, and his dad soon caught up. Beth and I continued our stride up the steep mountain pass.

Later, Beth told me the incident made her think about Mike's son, who would grow up without a father. She was so sad to think that the boy would have that void in his life, that no one would be there to give him courage and show him strength in the way only a father can.

Chapter 8
Clothes-less on the Mountain

Along the John Muir Trail, eight miles
and 3,000 feet up from the beginning
July 29, 2003

Half Dome is the trademark of Yosemite National Park. We came to a trail junction where groups of tourists ritualistically split from the John Muir Trail for the last leg of their Half Dome adventure. We planned to take the side trail up to Half Dome, but as we neared the trail junction, a dark, black cloud hovered low as if it had followed us and emerged like a stage prop, rumbling thunder. Dozens of tourists from the Half Dome trail hurried by, in too much of a hurry for small talk. As the day hikers skirted past, we alerted them about the bears. The real possibility of lightning striking on the exposed face we would traverse was enough to alter our plans of climbing Half Dome. The metal cables pounded into the rock for use as handles easily could become conductors of electricity if lightening struck. A drizzle began to fall as we stood at the trail junction, looking up at the clouds and down at our map.

"I think we should forget about the Half Dome hike and continue on," I said.

With a sigh of relief, Beth agreed. We had been hiking nearly four hours and only covered six miles. Seven miles remained if we were to reach our campsite destination, Sunrise High Sierra Camp.

We already had gained at least 3,000 feet in elevation since leaving Happy Isles. The elevation gain, combined with our full packs, kept us walking at a snail's pace. I had clipped along similar climbs in the Appalachians at a more rigorous pace, so I was frustrated. But we now were at elevations higher than any Appalachian mountain, and the thinner air was having more effect on me than I thought it would. Beth and I would take short breaks every quarter mile or so.

The rain had increased from a misty drizzle into a continuous shower. In spite of the tree cover, we were getting wet, and clouds blocked the sun. We stopped to put on our rain parkas, pump water from a nearby stream, and eat an energy bar. It was 4 p.m. We still had at least five miles to cover to reach camp. As I pulled my rain jacket and water bladder from my pack, something seemed to be missing. Then I realized my bag of clothes wasn't in my pack. I leaned my backpack up against a tree and frantically tore out everything with both hands. I tossed my 25-pound canister of food, sleeping bag, first-aid kit, assorted trinkets, and tent in every direction, hoping to find my bag of clothes tucked away somewhere. I didn't want to believe that I had actually left the bag containing all my clothes back where we started eight miles down the mountain. Beth and I had caught a ride on the Yosemite Valley shuttle bus to the start of the trail earlier in the day. In addition to our backpacks, we had carried several bags on board the bus that hadn't yet been tucked into our backpacks. One was my bag of clothes. The Englishman's comment began to reverberate in my mind: "You'll never bloody make it." We were at the beginning of an expedition in a mountain range that was notoriously unforgiving and could toss snow, sleet, hail, and rain unannounced. Without the right layers of clothing, one could easily succumb to hypothermia—a deadly scenario characterized by shivers, slurred speech, drowsiness, confusion, and, if not treated, death. We had climbed nearly 3,000 strenuous feet in elevation on one of the most vertical ascents of the entire John Muir Trail. We left the masses of tourists miles earlier. Going back down the mountain would be mentally defeating to our goal of walking the entire 221 miles.

Beth was collecting all the items as fast as I was discarding them. My pack now lay empty on the ground. I was chagrined. How could I, an accomplished hiker of the entire Appalachian Trail, be careless enough to leave my clothes behind? What a rookie move. I should have double-checked all our gear before departing. Beth sat down in the pouring rain with a defeated look on her face and tears welling up in the corners of her eyes. We had meticulously planned this trip for more than six months, and on Day One in the woods, this happens.

We were quiet, pondering our situation for several minutes. I had convinced Beth to abandon her amenities for a three-week expedition in the woods. I needed to collect myself and not allow a bag of clothes get in the way of ruining this once-in-a-lifetime adventure.

The rain eased to a mist. I calmly stuffed everything back in my pack and weighed the idea of hiking back down the mountain. Looking down the trail from where we had come, we could see a bearded man hiking toward us. The hiker was toting a heavy pack that towered above his head. He wore a navy blue windbreaker, one of those wide-collared jackets you see football coaches wear on the sidelines—not quite hiking material. He introduced himself as John as he dropped his pack from his shoulders, slinging it onto the ground. He explained that he, too, was planning to walk to Mount Whitney. Rivulets of sweat streamed down his face from the strenuous climb. He pulled out his water filter—a plastic cylinder with a filter inside—to refill his water supply from the stream we were standing next to. Animal urine and feces spread bacteria called Giardia, and hikers use filters, iodine, or boiling to kill these bacteria. In a scruffy, straining smoker's voice punctuated with hacking coughs, John explained that he was a engineer from Utah and he had just quit smoking pot after ten years. That's right, marijuana, not cigarettes like you expect most folks to say when they tell you they just quit smoking. As John pumped his water from the stream, I wondered whether there was a Pot-smokers Anonymous club out there that encouraged their members to tell everyone they quit smoking pot as part of the therapy. We introduced ourselves and gave a brief lowdown on our "Hike For Mike." We told John about our clothing situation.

"I left my bag of clothes on the shuttle bus down in Yosemite Valley, and walking 16 miles round-trip to recoup them is really daunting," I said.

As John continued pumping water, he suggested that we continue ahead another 12 miles to Tuolumne Meadows, and then catch a park shuttle bus back to the valley and check with lost and found for our clothes. Apparently, John had researched logistics more thoroughly than we had. He explained that he had hiked in Yosemite National Park many times.

We thanked John for the advice and continued toward our destination with new vigor, knowing we wouldn't have to slink back the way we came. Although we didn't have my clothes yet, we at least had a much more practical plan than backtracking. The worst-case scenario would be that I would have to buy some clothes at one of the park outfitter shops. We had the essentials to survive bad weather, so I would be fine for another day without more clothes. We left John at the stream. His cough grew fainter as we walked further along the trail and up the mountain. We never did run into John again. But his calm suggestion had motivated us and affirmed the notion that frustration doesn't help survival situations.

When we met John, it had been around 5 p.m. After viewing the map, we realized we still had five or six miles to go to Sunrise High Sierra Camp. We had barely averaged one and a half miles an hour. Although we were ascending one of the biggest climbs of the entire trek, I had anticipated at least a two-mile-per-hour pace. The 13-mile trek to the camp was turning into a give-it-all-you-got goal. We began to realize that we wouldn't reach camp until long after nightfall.

Most JMT hikers start in Yosemite Valley at 4,035 feet above sea level and hike south, primarily to avoid altitude sickness from the lofty elevations further south. Mount Whitney tops out at 14,496 feet. Many of the peaks along the southern half of the JMT reach above 12,000 feet. Starting in Yosemite would give us a natural adjustment to elevation. Altitude sickness is an unpleasant experience. You generally begin to feel the effects of altitude above 8,000 feet, and the higher you climb, the thinner the air gets and the harder it is to breathe. Some people such as myself are prone to altitude sickness. Symptoms include nausea, headaches, and loss of appetite. Sickness concerns aside, we were thankful we had started in Yosemite because of the opportunity to catch a shuttle bus back to locate my clothes.

We were still hiking below tree line and occasionally crossed creeks as we continued our trek further up the mountain toward the camp. The sun was creeping slowly down from the sky and would soon drop behind the mountain, leaving us to walk into the night. Beth and I stopped for a rest. I broke out the remaining cheese and summer sausage from our lunch earlier to quell our hunger until we reached camp.

Finally, the sun dipped behind the mountain, and the trail became more and more difficult to see. The wind kicked up. It howled in our ears as we approached a ridge near Sunrise Mountain. The rain had stopped, but the temperature seemed to be plummeting since the sun went down. We had goose bumps on our arms. As we neared the top, we stumbled across a young family—a man, woman, and their 11-year-old son. They were standing on the trail and debating whether or not to set up camp or continue on. They also had left from Happy Isles and planned to camp at Sunrise Camp. The reality was setting in that they were not going to make it before dark. They had rudimentary camping equipment. The father had a hatchet strapped to his belt. They were wearing jeans and flannels—not the recommended clothing for mountain trekking—but they seemed in good shape for such an adventure. Beth and I introduced ourselves as we rummaged through the top pouches of our packs to retrieve our headlamp flashlights—similar to what miners wear. I helped Beth put on her headlamp so she could turn it on when it became too dark to see.

The reality that our first night in the woods would be more on the adventuresome side and less on the romantic side began to take hold. For weeks, I had boasted to Beth how romantic this first night in the woods would be—our biggest adventure together, like the launch of a new vessel on its maiden voyage. We would leave all our worries behind and focus only on food, shelter, sleep—and a few other categories on Abraham Maslow's hierarchy of self-actualization—as we marched toward Mount Whitney.

Our decision to keep going until we reached Sunrise Camp must have inspired the family in their decision. They followed us up and over the ridge and walked with us most of the way. We marched into the night for quite some time. The beady eyes of nocturnal animals glowed and glared at us all along the trail. Beth clung close—more so than she had all day. We both were worried and wary that we might encounter more bears. They usually are more active at night. At times, it became difficult to see the trail, and we occasionally wondered whether we were still on the trail at all.

We grew tired. We became clumsy with our steps and would trip over rocks. Around 9:30 p.m., we emerged from the tree line into a grass-covered meadow. We could see a campfire across the meadow along the forest perimeter. As we marched in that general direction, we could see beams of flashlights bobbing around. Relief washed through us as we realized that we had finally reached our destination.

Chapter 9
Plan B

We trudged across the meadow. We followed the darting glow of flashlights like weary sea captains steering their ships toward lighthouses. The family had fallen behind, so Beth and I were alone. The smell of burning wood evoked warm memories of past camping trips. Throughout the Sierras, there are strict rules against campfires above 10,000 feet due to the risk of wildfires. We were at 9,300 feet. We filed along a narrow dirt path past several waist-high two-person backpacking tents as we searched for a place to set up our tent. Sandwiched between two other tents, we found a small, flat clearing large enough for us. We dropped our packs. I opened the main compartment of my backpack and pulled out our tent. With my headlamp lighting my field of vision, I unwrapped a sheet of plastic to cover the flat tent spot, and then I unraveled our tent. Moments later, we had a nylon-walled cave to crawl into. This would serve as our house for the next three weeks.

Beth excused herself, reluctantly grabbing her plastic bag of toilet tissue, and slipped away into the trees in search of a private spot to dig a cat-hole bathroom. I found a stream nearby and scooped up some water in my two-quart pan to boil for dinner. I pulled out our one-burner stove, attached it to the quart-sized white fuel canister, pumped it several times, turned on the burner, and flicked my lighter. A flame erupted, and a few moments later, it intensified into a hot blue. I placed the pan of water on the burner to boil. Beth returned from her bathroom excursion, unfolded our sleeping bags, and began blowing into the air nozzles of our Therm-a-Rest mattress pads. We fumbled in the dark for a coin to twist open a bear canister to retrieve a dinner to prepare. We settled on freeze-dried lasagna.

Moments later, dinner was ready. We sat in the dark, using our bear canisters as stools, headlamps on, eating from the same pouch of food. We took turns plunging our spoons into the pouch of lasagna, which we had situated in the pot for stability. I thought to myself that in a Neanderthal kind of way, this was romantic. Clothes-less man share dim meal with woman after long walk in woods.

After eating, I rinsed our spoons off, crammed the empty meal package back into the bear canister, and walked down the trail in search of a good bathroom spot. I could faintly make out the shape of a shed-sized building, which to my surprise turned out to be a bathroom. I returned to camp, grinning as I informed Beth that she could have gone in a real bathroom instead of the woods. Her makeshift bathroom probably was only 20 yards away from the real thing.

We crawled into our tent, and I fell asleep instantly. In the morning, I learned that Beth had drifted in and out of a light sleep, waking up to every little sound outside our nylon cave. At home, Beth makes frequent bathroom visits throughout the night. She never left the tent all night—frightened of encountering a bear or other creature that goes bump in the night.

The sun came over the mountain early, serving as nature's wake-up call. We both emerged from our tent. Beth immediately ran off to the bathroom. The smell of bacon and eggs hit my nose instantly as I gnawed on a granola bar and waited for our water to boil for coffee. In daylight, we could see the whole camp. Beyond a thin stand of bushes and trees stood several tent cabins similar to what we had stayed in the night before. There was even a solar-paneled shower house and water spigot. A group on a guided hike filled the cabins and was now eating the hot breakfast provided. All they had to carry on their backs were their clothes and lunch. Breakfast, dinner, and lodging were taken care of by a guide service. Although my taste buds were teased by the smell of their hot breakfast, we hadn't been out in the woods long enough to motivate a raid on their kitchen.

We began to meet the occupants of the tents surrounding us as we slowly packed up our gear. Two gray-haired men with beer bellies camped behind us—hiking buddies ever since their Boy Scout days. The sound of a tent zipper drew our focus next door as a young couple emerged with squinting eyes and mangled hair, not quite ready to pack up, let alone chat with their neighbors. We also spotted the family we had met, glad to see that they had arrived safely after us in the night. They sat in front of one of those large tents you see set up in the sporting goods department. It evoked some childhood memories of my domesticated car-camping trips with my family. Most everyone camped here was out for two to three days.

Today, we planned to hike 12 miles south to Tuolumne Meadows, where I would supposedly be able to get a shuttle bus ride back to Yosemite Valley to retrieve my bag of clothes. Beth and I got on the trail about 9 a.m. The sky was partly cloudy, and the sun was peering out.

After getting out of visual range of the other hikers, I hollered to Beth to hold up. I took off my pack, unclipped my pack straps, and retrieved a plastic bag containing our satellite phone. When Lewis and Clark set out to walk west into uncharted territory, they took what were considered at the time to be the most high-tech supplies available. By today's standards, a satellite phone was the most high-tech device to use in such a remote area. It provided instant, reliable communication. I could have phone reception anywhere in the world, as long as I was in a clearing. This gizmo even had the ability to give GPS grid coordinates if necessary. If satellite phones were available in Lewis and Clark's time, I guarantee they would have brought one along to report their findings to the president as they happened. For our expedition, this device would serve as our communication link with our webmaster as she updated the thousands of people following our hike. Respecting the "get away from it all" hikers, I waited until they were out of sight before pulling out our phone. I flipped the cigar-sized antenna out so it could signal up to an orbiting satellite. I dialed the lost-and-found office in Yosemite Valley, and in no time I was chatting with a park official on the other end. No clothing bag had been turned in, but the park official assured me she would check with the shuttle bus garage. She instructed me to call back when we reached Tuolumne Meadows. I then placed our first call to our webmaster. I updated her on the bear encounter, how we left my clothes back in Yosemite Valley, and that we were in good spirits. The same day, Georgia added our update to our website. Thousands were monitoring our progress and had been eager to get a report that we were on the trail and safe.

Distant snow-covered mountain peaks surrounded us. We would climb only a few hundred feet in elevation today in comparison to the 5,000 feet the day before. Surprisingly, neither of us were sore because we had trained properly and the miles seemed to fly by with the easy terrain. We walked through small meadows, dipping in and out of pine forest. We were in an area known as Cathedral Pass. A lake came into view below us—Cathedral Lake. We stopped for a picture and were mesmerized by the solitude we felt. There were no crowds, no parking lots or hot dog stands, just a beautiful bluish lake encased by an outer perimeter of mountains and an immediate perimeter of pine trees. The trail skirted around the lake, and a short hike later, we came to a trail junction with a side trail leading off to another lake. We passed a few backpackers out for a few days in the woods. They sure picked a beautiful spot.

The heat intensified as the morning sun peaked. We began to hear the all-too-familiar rumbling sound of cars that let us know that we were getting close to Tuolumne Meadows—another popular tourist destination in Yosemite National Park. The trail let out near the Tuolumne Visitors Center. We had walked 27 miles since beginning our hike at Happy Isles the day before. Beth and I were both eager to contact the lost-and-found back in Yosemite Valley. We found a pay phone on the outer front wall of the rustic, brown-painted visitor center. I placed the call while Beth meandered around. They had indeed located our clothing bag. The park official said I would have to claim it in person, which immediately sent us on a new adventure.

A park ranger inside the visitor center explained that we could catch a shuttle back to Yosemite Valley for 15 bucks one way. There was a domesticated campground down the road a mile that was a pickup point for the shuttle bus. Beth and I began walking along the road. Soon, we heard the grinding of a large diesel engine. A commercial-size bus slid to a halt. The door swung open, and the driver, a gray-haired, lean, healthy-looking man, shouted, "Where to?" We explained. He said to hop on and he would drop us off at the campstore and that he would return to the carryout because he was also the driver scheduled to navigate the shuttle bus to Yosemite Valley. In minutes, we arrived at the campstore. We had 30 minutes until he would return.

We decided that Beth would stay and set up camp at the campground, and I would catch the shuttle bus back. This made sense, instead of shelling out an additional $30 for Beth to sit on a bus for half a day. Taking advantage of the short time until the bus would return, we stepped over to the snack bar and ordered some food. We scarfed down cheeseburgers, fries, and milkshakes. Within minutes, the shuttle would arrive, so I pulled the tent from my pack and strapped it to the outside of Beth's pack. Other than having to assemble the tent, Beth would be able to relax for the rest of the day, with access to hot food, a store, and a pay phone, while I took the four-hour round trip bus ride.

Craig steered the bus into the half-circle parking lot in

front of the store right on schedule. I took all of my gear. Craig took my pack and loaded it below the cabin in the luggage compartment along with the gear of the half dozen other passengers. Craig was commandeering a full-size passenger bus with enough seating to accommodate at least 60 more folks than the few who boarded for the trip down the mountain. The riders had four to five rows of seats to themselves. I took a seat near the front of the bus.

We pulled onto the road in the direction of Yosemite Valley. For the next two hours, we wound down the mountain, dropping the 5,000 feet in elevation Beth and I had climbed yesterday. The road snaked along the mountain edge with mile-high views down into the valleys between the mountains. We were so far up in elevation that the raging rivers below looked like wispy threads. Other than the driver's precision, the only thing preventing the bus from dropping off the cliff's edge was a two-feet-high cement mortar wall. The driver casually referred to it as a psychological barrier and explained that the wall had no steel reinforcements and probably would break free with the pressure of a vehicle pushing into it. The driver had successfully eliminated any comfort that small wall had given us passengers. The tired riders startled in their seats and gulped with concern. The driver had effectively turned a run-of-the-mill bus ride into an adventure. Craig named several of the mountains as we passed and commented that he would love to look himself but thought we might appreciate it if his hands remained on the wheel and his eyes on the road. Occasionally, Craig would shout to us to look back to enjoy certain views. It was obvious that he had been doing this awhile. He was a class act of entertainment as we rode down the mountain.

I had taken a seat in the front of the bus so I wouldn't get sick from all the twists and turns. As long as I kept an eye on the road, I was fine. Craig explained that he had walked the Pacific Crest Trail in the '70s. He had a laid-back demeanor that one tends to get from enjoying his work. Craig has been working for Yosemite National Park ever since his PCT thru-hike. I complimented him on finding a career that immersed him in some of the same wild lands he hiked through. I told him that I had walked the Appalachian Trail. Craig began listing various names of hikers that he had met on his shuttle excursions who also had walked the AT, and wouldn't you know it, he had befriended a hiker I met on the AT.

Craig was an encyclopedia of information about the area. He knew the history of the roads, how some of the mountains got their names, and trivia about the wildlife in Yosemite. He mentioned that no one had ever been seriously injured or killed in the park by a bear. But every year it seemed that someone got injured by the mule deer. Mule deer are bigger than their whitetail cousins and try to avoid contact with humans. When tourists encroach on mule deer's personal space, they feel threatened and sometimes stand on their hind legs and strike with their front hooves. It can be lethal.

The bus stopped along a quiet, lonely road. Craig let a hiker on board who apparently worked for the park service. I introduced myself and inquired where he was hiking. The man bypassed my inquiry but did say he worked for the park service. He wouldn't disclose in what capacity, leading me to speculate that he must have been some kind of lawman looking for mischief in the forest. Either way, he apparently was on some sort of adventure, which to me makes life all that more enjoyable.

We reached Yosemite Valley, and Craig explained where to catch the next shuttle back to Tuolumne Meadows and that we would have a different driver and bus. I thanked Craig for the ride as he hoisted my pack from the luggage compartment and handed it to me. I slung my pack on and hurried over to the ranger dispatch office to claim my bag of clothes. A female ranger wearing the signature wide-rimmed gray hat greeted me in the dispatch office in the motor pool area of the park maintenance compound. I displayed my ID and signed a document, and she handed over my bag of clothes. I thanked the ranger profusely and darted back out the door to catch the one and only bus back leaving for Tuolumne Meadows.

The shuttle bus back to Tuolumne was loaded on a first-come, first-served basis. Quite a crowd was gathering at the bus stop, but it wasn't enough to fill the large bus that I had ridden in down the mountain. Several buses stopped, dropping off and picking up passengers for various routes. Then a smaller bus—almost a van—pulled in front of all of us. Everyone standing there began to eye the crowd, which would have fit easily into a standard-size bus but might not fit into this one. Everyone carried overstuffed backpacks. I was puzzled why the bus I rode from Tuolumne to Yosemite Valley had room for at least 60 but only carried a few passengers, and now with a crowd that could easily fill that larger bus, we had a van-bus designed to carry only half of us comfortably.

The driver stepped out, walked to the back of bus, opened the back door, and explained that we should pile our packs, stacking them on top of each other. Then she walked to the passenger door and explained that we would file in and fill the seats first. When the seats were full, the remaining passengers would file and fill the center aisle. No one thought we would all fit. There must have been at least 50 of us.

I was anxiously standing at the end of the line. Even though I had explained to Beth that I might get stuck without a ride until morning, I really didn't think I would have a problem getting back. My worry intensified that there wouldn't be enough room on the shuttle and Beth would be alone. She would be scared to death.

The passengers continued to file onto the bus until at last I boarded—or should I say I crammed myself aboard. I would have to stand for the entire two-hour ride up the mountain. The van had windows for the seated passengers to peer out at the surroundings, but the 20 of us standing butt to groin in the aisle had no view. As soon as the bus set in motion, I realized this was going to be a long ride. I clung to the handle attached to the roof and swayed with the snaky hairpin turns as the van crawled up the mountain. Several of us standing passengers turned a sickly white, no doubt causing the seated passengers to worry that we would empty our stomachs on them. This must be what cattle feel like, crammed into semi trailers on the way to slaughter. The driver knew this would be difficult for the standing passengers and pulled over several times to let us off to get fresh air and recover. I was thankful that I would soon be with Beth, and I realized how much better off she was by not having to deal with this ride. Finally, the van-bus pulled into the same half-circle drive I left hours earlier. We all piled off and exchanged goodbyes. We aisle-standing hikers had shared a bonding experience during our nauseating adventure. We grabbed our backpacks from the back door and walked off in our separate directions. Some were returning to their cars after a hike; some were planning to hike back to Yosemite; some were planning to camp. I was the only one on board walking the John Muir Trail.

Beth was standing outside the bus as if I were a child returning from his first day of school. She was worried that I didn't catch the bus—if she only knew how close I was to being left in the valley—and was scared that she would have to spend the night alone. She heard the bus gears grinding up the mountain road and ran from the campground.

We walked a few hundred yards along the berm of the road and into the campground, past RVs and pop-up campers, all the way to the designated tent area in the back of the campground. I could see our tent perched on a hill. Beth had established camp in an excellent spot. She had spent most of the time I was gone reading in the tent. She had ducked out of a lightning storm that had un-leashed itself almost immediately after I was gone.

"You were gone a long time. I was worried." Beth said.

"I have been on a bus all day. Trust me, sitting in the tent was a better experience than I just had riding down and up the mountain," I said.

We pulled out our stove and prepared a freeze-dried dinner. Plan B had worked. We had my clothes and everything we needed to make it to our halfway re-supply point. It felt as if our journey was starting all over again.

Chapter 10
We Know You're Up There

Donohue Pass, 37 miles from Happy Isles
July 31, 2003

The morning light illuminated our tent walls. We woke naturally without the beep of an alarm clock and the demand of a workload. All we had to do was walk on our own schedule. The inner walls of our tent were covered in beads of moisture—condensation from our breath. I slipped on my pants, shirt, socks, coat, hat, and sandals, then unzipped the tent door. The sky was cloudy but not rainy. I stepped over to my pack and glanced at the thermometer dangling from a pocket zipper. It was 60 degrees.

I unclipped the chain and security clip to unfasten the bear-proof steel container—there was one at every campsite—that protected our food during the night. I had left our stove on the picnic table overnight. I gave it a few pumps, turned on the burner, flicked my lighter, and got foot-high flames. I adjusted the burner down to a sky-blue flame and in no time at all, I had a pot of water spitting bubbles for coffee. Beth climbed out of her sleeping bag and dashed off to use the bathroom, taking advantage of one of her last opportunities to use flush toilets and a sink. These facilities were by no means luxurious in comparison to home. There was no hot water and no shower stall, and a large sign above the sink read: "NO BATHING OR WASHING DISHES IN SINK."

I poured some coffee grounds from a plastic bag into a foil-screen coffee maker, held it over our coffee mug, and slowly poured hot water from our pan through the grounds. As I sat sharing sips of morning joe with Beth, I pulled some food from our bear canisters for our daily snacks and lunch. Meanwhile, Beth stuffed our sleeping bags into their sacks and deflated our mattresses. We were working naturally as a team. It felt good. In between sips of coffee, I took down the tent, pulled out the stakes and the poles, and rolled it up by squeezing out the air. I stuffed it into my pack.

With jolts of caffeine in our veins and granola bars in our bellies, we were on the trail by 8 a.m. Dozens of other hikers were coming alive from their tents as we slipped into our packs, picked up our trekking poles, and walked on. We had camped at 8,650 feet. Altitude sickness can take effect above 8,000 feet. I had a minor headache and a nauseated feeling—both signs of altitude sickness. We stopped along the trail so I could take a few ibuprofen. We continued walking, mostly in shaded forest. We encountered an organized group of hikers that was part of the High Sierra circuit. A woman in the hiking group asked about our "Hike For Mike" shirts. Beth talked about our depression awareness mission, what happened to Mike, and the mental and physical health aspects of hiking. The group took interest in our journey and planned to check out our website. After swapping trail talk for a few minutes, we continued on in separate directions.

The trail wormed out into a meadow of tall grass that was sprinkled with daisies and purple wildflowers. We began to parallel a mountain stream, the Lyell Fork of the Tuolumne River on our left, with car-size boulders and stands of trees leading up to a mountain ridge on our right. As long as I have known Beth, she has loved flowers—all kinds, although tulips and Gerbera daisies are her favorites. We stopped for a short break.

We had used red Gerber daisies at our wedding because tulips had been out of season in August. Mike couldn't make it to our wedding. He and his wife were expecting the birth of their son within weeks of our wedding day. They didn't want to risk the five-hour drive from Chicago to Miami University in Ohio, our alma mater and the site of our wedding. Five days into our honeymoon, we got word of the birth of their son while we were in Asheville, North Carolina. We toasted Mike's new son that night.

As we started strolling again, I felt as if we were being watched. As it turns out, we were. A yellow-bellied marmot was perched on a rock and was checking out Beth and me. He was plump with a squirrelly, curious face, and his fur was yellow and brown. He was about the size of a raccoon. Marmots live throughout the Sierras, and this little guy seemed to be posing for a picture. I pulled out my camera and walked toward him but he scurried beneath the rock. As I walked around to where he had slipped away, another marmot popped his head up on the other side of the rock. When I walked toward the other marmot, the first marmot reappeared. I think they were playing a game with me. I managed to take a few quality pictures.

We still were developing our stride. My pace was quicker than Beth's on the level sections of the trail. We wandered along under partly cloudy skies. The trail was a well-worn path of cocoa-brown dirt, and it was easily identifiable among the knee-high grass. We emerged from the dense tree cover into a meadow encased by mountains.

You can always tell when you're entering the backcountry by the number of people you encounter, the gear they carry, and the types of activities you witness. We were in Lyell Canyon, not more than a few miles from Tuolumne Meadows. Two hikers walking toward us came into view. They were returning to civilization after a few nights in the backcountry, and their packs were stuffed twice as much as Beth's and mine. Several fly fishermen in rubber waders negotiated the creek as we trekked by.

We rock-hopped across Ireland Creek, which invoked a conversation about thoughts of one day walking across Ireland, Beth's ancestral homeland. As we approached the far reaches of Lyell Canyon, we passed a distant summit named after Amelia Earhart, who was the first female to fly solo across the Atlantic but who vanished during an attempt to fly around the world. In a way, I thought the peak symbolized Beth's courage to undertake this maiden voyage of her own.

As we neared the far reaches of the canyon, we both gazed up at a distant waterfall. It darted off the top of a forested ridge and ran down a treeless granite rock slope like spilling white paint. We could see several large tents off in the tree line, which we suspected marked Lyell Fork Base Camp.

Beth and I reached the far end of the meadow, which was as large as 20 football fields encased by distant, smoky-colored, snow-speckled mountains. A man rounded the bend in front of us and headed in our direction. This guy was rather tall, lurching in at 6-foot-4, easy. He had gray hair escaping out from the edges of his baseball cap. Some sort of stick protruded from the top of his backpack like an antenna. As we closed in on each other, my eyes locked on to the object in his pack, and I realized it was a golf club.

"Good morning! Is there a golf course nearby?" I asked

"The winds are in my favor up here," the man replied.

The man stopped and smiled, displaying several gaps where his front teeth were missing. The skin around his eyes was wrinkled and leathery. His face was a deep copper color common to those who spend lots of time above the trees in mountain country. Before continuing along, he allowed us to take his picture while he practiced a swing with his 9 iron.

Beth and I agreed to stop for a break before leaving the flat canyon and beginning our big climb of the day. We were around 9,000 feet and would ascend over an 11,056-foot mountain at Donohue Pass. The trail profile in our guide-book showed a spike icon that looked like a heart monitor, indicating a serious incline that spanned several miles. A look at our topographical maps confirmed that we soon would begin our ascent and that this flat meadow walking was about to end. We found a log that looked comfortable enough to sit on with views of the meadow behind us. We couldn't see any-thing up ahead, just a forested mountain spiking up in front of us. This probably was the best time to rest. We dropped our poles, released our pack straps, and let the packs drop to the ground. We grabbed our bagels, peanut butter, and honey and sat down on the log. We gazed back at the way we had come as we ate our snacks. Beth felt as if something was watching us while we sat there. She had been a little nervous about bears since our earlier encounter. We were on display on the open meadow for all the critters to see.

Eventually, we stood up and walked over to the packs. I grabbed my pack by its threaded handle with my left hand near the center of the top, picked it up as if I was going to curl it, and then swung around, slipping my right arm in the shoulder strap while leaning forward and slipping my left arm through the other shoulder strap. Beth was attempting to imitate my pack mount, but she hadn't quite figured out how to sling her pack the way I did. I had perfected this procedure during my five months on the Appalachian Trail. I finished securing my hip belt and helped Beth mount her pack.

The level terrain was behind us, and our pace slowed. Our trekking poles served as a stairway railing. We stuck them into the trail with each step and pushed off for some added torque. We climbed for a while then stopped to look back at the meadow. The stream we had walked along in the canyon looked like a small, shiny snake winding through a flat meadow. It U-turned back and forth across the meadow, stopping short first at one mountain base and then the other, until it faded from view into the pine trees.

We ran into a hiker standing on the trail. He was leaning forward with his hands on his knees as if he was about to vomit, his pack still on. His face was as white as milk, and he wore a sickly frown. He said he had altitude sickness and was taking it easy. He was with a group of hikers that we would soon encounter up ahead. We felt bad for the guy, but we had miles to go. As Beth and I passed him, the sick hiker noticed my AT 2,000-miler patch sewn onto the back of my pack.

"Did you walk the AT?" he asked.

"Yep, in 1998," I responded.

"I did it in '97," he called back as he stood up from his hunched-over position.

We talked about the AT for a few minutes as Beth rolled her eyes. She had been in this predicament of listening to me engage in AT banter and fearing that I would wrap myself in a lengthy dialogue of whom-did-you-hike-with, what-trails-have-you-done-since, has-it-changed-your-life, etc. She wanted to keep our momentum going and use the energy from our break and snack to climb Donahue Pass. I noticed her impatience as she kept rotating and clicking her hiking sticks on the rocky ground. I took Beth's cues and abruptly ended our AT conversation, but not without first taking off my pack and offering my AT brother some trail magic of ibuprofen to help with his altitude sickness. Trail magic is an act of kindness one receives from a complete stranger on the trail.

We climbed all morning. We could hear thunder claps as coal-black clouds bunched together nearby. The trees were becoming sparse, the trail more rocky. Eventually, we found ourselves walking in the open without the cover of trees, fully exposed to the elements.

The thunderclaps increased in decibels as the dark clouds hovered above us. It posed a real danger. We were somewhere around 10,000 feet walking along a shoulder-width trail on a narrow ledge, with a rock mountain wall on our right and a death-promising drop-off down a steep rock embankment on the left. We had nothing to protect us from a lightning strike, and we were the tallest objects on the trail—basically the lightening rods of the mountain. Suddenly, rain splattered from the sky. Hard bolts of water pelted us as brilliant flashes of lightning and slamming thuds of thunder simultaneously lit up the sky and rumbled the ground below us.

"Beth, let's back down from here until the storm passes," I shouted above the hissing rain.

We turned around and began descending from the way we came in search of tree cover. We moved quicker than we had all morning. The trees began to increase in numbers around us. As we walked, a flash of lightning lit up our surroundings as if someone had struck a match in a dark cave, and a loud crack of thunder snapped. We were in the heart of the storm, and we were scared.

"Beth, drop your pack, leave your poles, and grab your pack cover," I yelled over the whipping wind and rain. I unclipped my hip belt and let my pack drop to the ground. Our trekking poles were made of metal, and electricity easily could shoot up the poles and into our bodies. I frantically unzipped my pack and grabbed my pack cover. We left our packs and poles on the side of the trail and continued down the mountain, searching desperately for a dense population of trees to demote us from the status of tallest fools on the mountain.

Without our packs, we trotted along, dropping considerably in elevation. The lightning and thunder were snapping and growling bursts of light, as if God were taking flash photos. I stopped, my eyes panning the area for a stand of trees. Beth was quiet, and she looked concerned. The trail was still thin and rocky, but at least we were below some sparse tree cover. I selected a group of pine trees off the trail on a hillside and unfolded my pack cover several feet from the base of one of the shorter trees.

"Beth, we need to sit on our pack covers with our hands on our knees and our heads between our legs," I shouted.

I positioned myself, and Beth copied. The idea was to make yourself as small as possible while preventing an electrical current from shooting down a tree and striking us.

In July, just before our expedition, the media airwaves erupted with a story of a group of climbers in Wyoming that were struck by lightning. One climber died, and several were injured. They were caught in a lightning storm above the tree line. The Wyoming incident was fresh in my mind, and we were in similar terrain. I wasn't taking any chances.

We sat on our pack covers in a position similar to the pose schoolchildren are instructed to assume during tornado drills. Thunder and lightning pounded and zapped all around us, as if the storm was looking for us. We must have sat there for 30 minutes. We were separated from all of our gear, which lay up the mountain where we had left it on the trail.

I wondered if the golfer we had encountered earlier had taken his 9 iron off his pack.

Finally, the decibels of thunder decreased, and the bright flashes vanished from view as the black clouds slowly made their way off the mountain and headed for another range. We stood up, wet and cramped from our uncomfortable sitting position. As we walked back up the mountain to where we had left our packs, I wondered if we would be dealing with this storm all day. Soon, we would be far above tree line—too far to make a mad dash below the trees. We found our packs and poles unscathed where we had left them. I slung my pack on and helped Beth with hers. We trudged slowly up the trail, feeling like retreating soldiers ordered back to retake lost ground.

The dynamics of our relationship were different out here than in our typical domesticated life. Instead of having our usual discussion before making decisions, I had barked orders to Beth on what to do during the storm. I was serving a dual role as Beth's husband and guide during this expedition. I had led dozens of groups on hikes in the Appalachians over the years. I'm a believer in "hiking your own hike" unless there is danger or I have a good solution to a problem someone is having. I had committed to Beth that I would make sure we got to Mount Whitney—safely—and I was bound and determined to make sure we did. However, I also didn't want our relationship out here to be a "Yes, Jeff" set-up, and I'm quite sure there would be mutiny aboard my little ship if I even tried to pull a move like that. This adventure was just beginning, and it already was steering us into new areas of our relationship.

Shortly after mounting our packs and moving along the trail, we heard voices. Soon, a train of people on horseback came into view. The lead rider—the guide—wore a cowboy hat and a black raincoat similar to what old Civil War photographs showed the generals wearing. The guide was an attractive female, with long, wavy brown hair coming out from beneath her hat. Beads of rainwater rolled off her parka. It was obvious this group had endured the same storm at a higher elevation. I was impressed with the horses' ability to hold riders on their backs while negotiating a rocky and narrow footpath along a mountain edge. Beth and I stepped up onto some rocks off the trail to let the horses pass. The riders greeted us as they ambled past. The first horse was followed by six horse-size mules, their riders sporting round safety helmets.

We hopscotched up toward Donohue Pass to avoid stepping in the fresh dung with which the mules and horse had ornamented the trail. We could now see Donohue Pass, a treeless, gray, rocky peak covered with large blankets of snow. The sun peered out from the clouds, briefly rewarding us with hopeful thoughts that this weather soon would pass. Although we had meticulously prepared for this journey, we had no control over the elements. The lightning storm was a reminder that we were ultimately in God's hands. The immortal side of our adventure was clear and present. We were being watched over. Our four-boot "Hike For Mike" team zigzagged up a series of exposed narrow switchbacks, aggressively climbing in elevation as we tackled Donohue Pass.

Beth says that although I had talked before about the spiritual side of the wilderness and the outdoors, it was at that point that she realized what I meant. She had always associated running with her spirituality, and now her spiritual horizon had expanded to include hiking.

Chapter 11
Lions and Rivers and Boy Scouts, Oh My

Rush Creek Camp, 41 miles from Happy Isles,
July 31, 2003

My biggest fear is drowning. When I was three, I fell into the deep end of my grandmother's swimming pool. I drifted to the bottom, sucking water. By sheer luck, my uncle happened to be looking out the attic window of my grandmother's house while he was sneaking a cigarette. He saw me sitting in the pool and ran from the house, dove into the pool, yanked me from the water, and pumped my belly until I started coughing. It was one instance in which smoking actually saved a life. But I had been fearful of drowning ever since. The John Muir Trail winds around hundreds of lakes and fords through scores of mountain streams. The relatively few footbridges are limited to the most dangerous river crossings. I knew that fording mountain streams would be necessary to make this journey. If it wasn't for the rave reviews and stunning photos, I might have chosen a different trail just to avoid the river fords—perhaps a trail designed by someone with the same fear of drowning as me, which no doubt would include bridged water crossings over every creek, stream, and river. Beth wasn't exactly an Olympic swimmer, either.

We continued climbing Donohue Pass. The trail leveled off into a rather flat meadow with snow-covered peaks looming in every direction. The rain stopped, but the sky remained a charcoal gray. The trail disappeared at the bank of a wide stream and continued again on the other side, as if the stream had flooded the trail. But that wasn't the case. The trail architects intentionally sent it through the stream. This was our first river ford of the trip.

The guidebook, other hikers, and several journals we had read warned of several river fords that can be dangerous. In preparation for our trip, I insisted that Beth and I practice river-crossing techniques. We forded our living room from the front door into the dining room on several dry runs and then purposefully forded unnecessary mountain streams during a practice hike in the Great Smoky Mountains. We practiced placement of walking sticks for stability, how to cross with more than one person, and how to find a safe spot to cross. Having a plan is half the battle.

We stood anxiously on the bank and studied the currents, looking for the best place to cross. Just 20 yards down, the water disappeared into a waterfall that plummeted down a rock ledge. Upstream, a man had just stepped off the embankment on the other side of the river. He staggered to keep his balance, knocked off center by the hydraulics of the current as he slowly forded thigh-deep water. He climbed onto our embankment and then immediately turned to watch his son follow the same route. He also made a safe passage through the stream. A train of pack mules approached the river directly across from where we stood. A man on horseback led the mules across, their bellies submerged in the water. No one seemed in danger, and that gave us peace of mind. We shed our packs, pulled off our boots and socks, strapped on our sandals, tied our boots on the outsides of our packs, slung our packs back on, and crossed where the mules had. The water was frigid. Using our trekking poles for stability against the strong current, we easily crossed to the opposite embankment without any mishaps. We sat on the bank as we secured our socks and boots back on our feet.

We eagerly followed the trail, knowing we were encroaching on the summit of Donohue Pass. We walked to the edge of the meadow and climbed up a rock-laden, narrow trail that switched back and forth along a barren granite mountain ridge. When we reached the ridge, we thought we had reached the summit, but we realized as we stood panting in the thinning air that the trail continued through a rock-riddled flat landscape toward a distant, snow-covered peak. The wind kicked up with a chill as we continued our march.

A leaf-green hiking tent stood out against the lifeless-looking meadow several yards off the trail. It was butted up to a large rock that served as a wind barrier. A young man and woman who perched on a nearby rock were bundled in gloves and hooded windbreakers. We talked briefly. They had set out from Yosemite the same day as we to hike the entire JMT. They were so impressed with the snow-covered mountain vistas in every direction that the teeth-chattering wind and nauseating elevation didn't faze them. We estimated that we were less than a mile from Donohue Pass.

Other than flying in the pressurized cabin of a commercial jet, I have only been this high in elevation one other time in my life. Nearly 12 years ago, my good friend Brian and I had motored out west with ambitions of hiking in the Rockies. We arrived in Rocky Mountain National Park only to find that all the backcountry permits were already issued. A park ranger had suggested going north out of the national park boundary into the Roosevelt National Forest. "You guys will have the trail all to yourselves," he had said. We registered for a weeklong backcountry permit and headed out. We made a naive error common to easterners used to walking in lower elevations. We ascended to 13,000 feet on the first day because the terrain was smooth-packed horse trails that gradually zigzagged up the mountain. The next morning, I felt sick to my stomach, like I was going to vomit, and I had a headache throbbing in my ears and forehead—similar to a bad hangover. Aspirin and ibuprofen didn't suppress the headache. It wasn't until I had descended in elevation a few days later that I began to feel better. I had altitude sickness, which could have been prevented had I ascended gradually.

With my awful altitude experience permanently encoded in my memory, much like what an adult remembers of childhood chicken pox, I wanted to work up gradually to camping at high elevations on our JMT hike. Our goal of the day was to safely get up and over the 11,056-foot summit of Donahue Pass. We would then drop in elevation back near 10,000 feet to camp. The higher you climb in elevation, the less oxygen is available for you to breathe.

We were fortunate that the rash of thunderstorms had chosen to hover over a distant mountain for a while. The higher we climbed, the more surreal the terrain became. I felt as if we were climbing into the clouds. I half-hoped we wouldn't get snagged by a low-flying 747 plagued by low visibility. The wind died down as we moved along. Snow-covered boulder fields surrounded the trail in every direction. How wild this was to be walking among snow in the middle of summer. We played a bit, dropping our packs and throwing snowballs at each other. Some patches of snow were colored a reddish brown from a protozoan (a living cell) that actually lives in the snow.

We reached Donohue Pass in the early afternoon. It was our highest elevation yet and marked the end of Yosemite National Park for the rest of our journey. A wooden plaque nailed to a log post proclaimed this was the Ansel Adams Wilderness Area. Looking back the way we had come, we saw a sign denoting the park boundary of Yosemite National Park. Boulders were strewn about as far as the eye could see. A cloud clung to the mountain and fogged up all the views. No one but Beth and I stood on the mountain pass. I thought it might be what the terrain of an uninhabitable planet is like. No trees or animals seemed to exist. Scattered boulders and rocks surrounded us by the millions. The lonely howl of wind roared in our ears, and we had nothing but each other's company to keep from getting spooked. This summit climate was a vastly different feel than most of the mountain summits along the Appalachian Trail.

Donohue Pass was the second of ten mountain passes Beth and I would summit before tackling the final and highest summit of the JMT: Mount Whitney. The further we trekked south from Yosemite, the more remote the trail became. The elevations were climbing steadily, and the trail seemed to become increasingly rugged. Already, the masses of tourists had dissipated down to a trickle of well-outfitted hikers. We were in territory that the average windshield tourist would never see. We wouldn't cross another road until the end of the hike.

In addition to spanning three national parks, the John Muir Trail also journeys through the Ansel Adams and John Muir wilderness areas, part of Inyo National Forest. Adams introduced the Sierra Nevada mountains to the world with his famous black-and-white photography of the breathtaking views. Several of his famous photographs were taken along the John Muir Trail.

Since leaving Yosemite Valley three days ago, we had walked approximately 35 miles.

Beth held her arms up in a victory V standing next to the park boundary sign as I snapped her picture. This was a well-earned accomplishment. Celebrating the little successes along the way would help get us to Mount Whitney.

As soon as I had zipped my camera back in its pouch, a grayish cloud hovering above dispensed icy specks of sleet. They smacked us with a cold sting as the specks melted into beads of water on our exposed arms. We dropped our packs, pulled out our rain parkas, slipped them on, remounted our packs, and began descending on the opposite side of Donohue Pass. The bills on our ball caps deflected the ice from our eyes.

We had some of the best clothing designed for hikers. Cotton is a big no-no on the trail. The only two cotton items we carried were our ball caps and bandannas. Cotton retains moisture. If worn in moderate temperatures during extreme physical activities, it will hold perspiration against your skin and cause irritation similar to a baby's diaper rash. In mountain climates with fluctuating temperatures, moisture-soaked cotton can quickly cool and chill your body's core temperature, resulting in hypothermia. Polypropylene, Capilene, nylon, silk, and wool all are used as mountaineering alternatives to cotton. Some of these high-tech fabrics actually wick the moisture away from your skin, helping to keep the body temperature stable. Layering is essential in mountain climbing, but if any of the layers are cotton, the layering is useless.

We were wearing synthetic nylon hiking shorts that could be converted to long pants by zipping on the lower leg halves. We had nylon boot coverings—called gaiters—clipped on our boot strings that sealed off the boot rims and prevented debris and moisture from entering through our socks. Our long-sleeved parkas were made of breathable Gore-Tex, and we wore our "Hike For Mike" polypropylene synthetic shirts underneath. The temperature was in the 40s. As long as we kept moving, we stayed warm. Beth had an "I want a hot chocolate" look on her face.

The sleet was constant as we descended off the pass and rapidly dropped in elevation. Beth led the way. I followed. My mind was off in random thoughts, far removed from the trail. I wasn't paying attention, assuming Beth was comfortable leading. She stopped suddenly in panic. She spun around, looked back to me, and said, "I don't think we're on the trail."

I snapped out of my daydream and looked around. Somehow we had left the trail and were now walking across endless boulder fields. Unlike the Appalachian Trail, which is marked the entire way with painted white blaze streaks every few hundred yards, the John Muir Trail is marked only at intersections with other trails. The trail is obvious, though, and hard to lose as it is at least three feet wide in most places and well worn, with rocks piled up along the edges. But we had been walking through boulder fields with deceiving worn spots, which can easily mislead a trekker.

I couldn't imagine getting lost up here in the harsh elements and wide-open space. We could march on for days without finding civilization. We panned the area, walking in a big loop in search of the trail. We were on a sloping mountainside strewn with rocks and some sparse patches of grass. I tried not to overreact. After all, I was the guide in our party. I asked Beth to stay in one spot as I backtracked up the pass, my eyes scanning every inch of ground for the trail. I looked back occasionally to make sure I could still see Beth. This way, I could keep a sense of direction. About fifty yards up the mountain, I found the trail. It was vague in direction and appeared as a junction with another trail, which is probably where we got off course. I waved Beth up the mountain and she backtracked to my position. We then resumed our descent along the JMT.

The sleet subsided. We were now wet from sweat condensed between our bodies and rain parkas. The trail leveled off to a marshy meadow with numerous shallow creek crossings easy enough to hop the rocks across. Alpine forest once again sprinkled the landscape. Bright orange wildflowers adorned the grassy meadow. Water smacked up from beneath our boots, telling us that this area was too boggy to make camp. We came to a creek too swift and wide to hop rocks across. We dropped our packs, took off our rain parkas, secured them to our packs, and donned our sandals.

I pulled out our map and guidebook to orient myself with our location. The guidebook profile of the John Muir Trail shows a chart of each mountain pass and valley that looks like a heartbeat on a cardio computer monitor. Donohue Pass looked like the major heartbeat for the entire first half of our journey. Another grid indicated the elevation, and the scale across the bottom of the chart indicated the miles. The profile showed a sharp drop from Donahue Pass, a 45-degree descent of at least 1,000 feet in elevation over the course of three to four miles. I studied the map, and based on the creek crossings we just navigated, I concluded we were near 10,000 feet.

As I stood up from the rock I had been resting on, my eyes honed in on a set of animal tracks in the mud on the bank of the stream. It shot a warning signal straight to the oh-no part of my brain. I crouched down for a closer look and realized that whatever left the tracks was much bigger than a bunny or a marmot. These tracks looked like the paw prints of a large dog—a large, fist-size paw pad with four thumb-size toe imprints but no claw imprints. I hadn't seen any Great Danes on the trail. As a matter of fact, dogs are forbidden on most of the trails in the national parks. These tracks were fresh—still wet, in fact—and had all the characteristics of the tracks of a large mountain lion.

The mountain lion is the last remaining predator and carnivore in the Sierra with the capability of hunting man. In many ways, mountain lions are more feared than bears and wolves because of their stealth and prowess. Sightings are rare because they live and travel alone. They stalk and ambush their prey, biting the back of the neck. They primarily feed on mule deer, elk, and sheep. Taking down a mule deer or an elk is no easy feat. Mule deer are larger than their whitetail cousins, and some weigh more than 300 pounds. An animal that can prey on deer of this size is quite capable of hunting man. In January 2004, as I wrote this chapter, two bicyclists were attacked—one fatally and the other seriously—by a mountain lion in Orange County, not far from where Beth and I spotted these tracks. According to the California Department of Fish and Game, more than half of California is considered mountain lion country. There are 400 incident reports filed annually involving human encounters with mountain lions in California alone, though fatalities are rare. Other states have large lion populations, including Oregon, Washington, Colorado, Wyoming, and Montana.

These lions are shorthaired and tan in color, resembling giant domestic cats. They also are called catomounts, pumas, panthers, and cougars. They can be as large as eight feet long from nose to tip of tail and can weigh up to 180 pounds. They prefer to go for the jugular vein while simultaneously attempting to break the neck, with the hope of feeding off the prey for several days until vermin join the feast. Warnings posted in Yosemite and all along the John Muir Trail warn hikers not to leave children unattended and not to hike alone.

There was something about the idea of actually being stalked by a wild animal that raised hair on my neck, but at the same time it added to the adventure. I might be lower on the food chain out here in mountain lion country. My negotiating skills would be useless with a mountain lion. I couldn't reason with it or sign a treaty specifying territories, rules, and limits. If a lion were to pursue Beth and me as food, it would be an all-out fight to survive.

I didn't want to cause Beth any alarm, so I stood up and attempted to divert my focus to something else before she caught on. But she had been watching me hover over the prints, and she knew exactly what was up. Some friends had joked with Beth before we departed not to fall far behind me for risk of being attacked by mountain lions. This thought didn't sit well with her and led to several lengthy conversations with me about the risk of a mountain lion attack. I convinced Beth that she would be fine—as long as she didn't fall too far behind.

"No big deal, Beth. They don't bother people in groups," I remarked in as relaxed a tone as I could muster as I walked away from the lion imprints. The risk of actually being attacked by a mountain lion supposedly is more remote than being struck by lightning or falling victim to many other natural disasters. But lion attacks do happen, and being out here with our minds reeling with possibilities, it was easy to become frightened.

Beth was silent, obviously pondering our safety. We continued our descent from Donahue Pass. The decline became more severe; it now was a dramatic roller-coaster-like angle. From our visual vantage point several hundred feet up on a ridge, we had seen a powder-blue tent down in what appeared to be a flat area, and it seemed we would reach that area soon. It was late afternoon, and we would need to find a campsite soon. We had been on the trail for eight hours. On our descent, I had to use the facilities, so we stopped along the trail. I slipped off my pack and dropped down a pine-covered embankment, leaving Beth alone on the trail with our packs. As I crouched down relieving myself, I suddenly realized how vulnerable we were to a lion attack. If a lion had been stalking us right then, it could have pounced easily from a nearby tree onto either one of us with its thick claws and razor-sharp teeth. Either of us could be dragged away without the other knowing. Even worse, if the lion decided to catch me relieving myself, the headlines would be a huge embarrassment. I hurriedly finished up and climbed back up to Beth. She was perched atop her pack, seemingly relaxed and content with the words of safety I had preached a while ago.

The trail continued down a steep descent on a narrow, zig-zagging switchback. The scattered trees turned into patches of forest canopy the further we descended. The blue tent I saw from high on the ridge was within 50 yards of where we stood. The trail leveled off with the promise of some possible campsites.

Burning wood smoldered in our nostrils. I hoped the smell was from a campfire and not a "contained" forest fire that had burned out of control. As we leveled off, we could see smoke puffing up from the center of a cluster of tents. Young boys were all about, sitting on logs and rocks that had been ar-ranged near a fire. Several men—the apparent guides—sat in their own circle separated from the boys. We waved, and several of them waved back. We stopped to look at our maps. One of the men from the group stood up and approached us. Another man followed him. They introduced themselves proudly as the leaders of a California-based Boy Scout troop. The leader, Dan, wore a brown Indiana Jones hat with a wide brim and a wool checkered flannel coat. He looked more like a cattle rancher than a Boy Scout leader. A second man ac-companying him wore the latest brand-name hiking gear.

"Where did you hike in from?" asked Indiana Dan.

"Yosemite," I replied. "We're walking the John Muir Trail."

Dan perked up. "Aw, I'd love to hike the JMT. We are hiking out of the backcountry tomorrow. We've been out for two days."

"Dan, would you mind if we found a camp nearby?"

"No, be our guests, if you don't mind the noise from the boys."

I didn't want to tell them that I would feel much safer

from lions there than if we found a remote camping spot. I didn't want to make Beth uneasy by talking about this.

"Rush Creek is just around the bend in the trail," the high-tech hiking dad chimed in.

"Thanks, guys," I replied.

The men walked back over to their fire ring, and Beth and I began searching for a spot to pitch our tent—far enough from the boys to give us some privacy, but close enough that they could hear our bloody-murder screams should the lion that made the paw prints pay us a surprise visit. There is something genuine and good-natured about fathers leading Boy Scouts into the woods. It's nostalgic, like a Norman Rockwell painting. The boys looked like they ranged in age from about 11 to 15. I figured we were in good company.

We found a flat, grass-covered spot 30 yards from the tree-shaded stream embankment. Our maps indicated that we were at 9,640 feet in elevation, which explained why the Scouts had a blazing bonfire. I had read in several JMT Web journals that the rangers were savvy at spotting fires above 10,000 feet. We had trekked 16 miles from Tuolumne Meadows. Beth and I worked as a team setting up camp. We tied a clothesline between two trees to hang our wet clothes. We ambled downstream far out of view of the boys to clean up. The water was bone-chilling. I stepped in up to my knees, splashing off the rest of my body with one of the traditional standing stream baths. Beth sat on the bank cupping water in her hands and splashing herself off, not willing to risk numbing herself with cold water. She pulled out a foil pack of wet naps, pulling one from the pack and wiping her skin. Layers of dirt darkened the tiny white towel.

We put on our campsite clothes—T-shirts and shorts—

which we donned only after cleaning up for the night. We put our fleece jackets and hats over our clean outfits to stay warm. I cooked up some macaroni & cheese for dinner. The sun peeked out as it set, and a hint of blue sky emerged from behind a gray cloud. We returned to the stream to wash our camp pot and pump drinking water. I was using the same pump filter that I had on my Appalachian Trail expedition. I had used this filter to pull water from small streams down-river from pig farms and mud puddles without ever getting sick, so I had come to rely on any water that passed through it.

The Scout leader with all the high-tech hiking gear stopped by our tent on his way back from the stream.

"You are both welcome to join us around our campfire," he said.

"Thanks. We might do that," I replied.

Beth didn't want to go anywhere, but she also didn't want to be left alone in the tent if I walked over to the fire. So she came along.

Beth later told me that the campfire made her think of Mike. When she was a graduate student at Miami University of Ohio, Mike had brought his wife and stepdaughter to visit her, along with another brother, Brian. In the tradition of their family outings as kids, Mike brought along camping gear, and they all had gone camping at Hueston Woods State Park. They had sat around a campfire and relived their child-hood traditions of making pie-iron pizzas and s'mores. They had played cards into the wee hours, and they all slept in a giant tent.

Beth and I sat and talked with the Scouts for a while. They were a troop from Orange County, not too far from Mount

Whitney. The boys were in high spirits and seemed to be enjoying their hike. They also were excited to hike out of the backcountry the next day.

On our walk back to our tent, Beth and I stopped in front of the tent where four of the chaperons sat.

"You guys have a good bunch of Scouts," I told them.

"Thanks. We enjoy getting the boys out here once or twice a year," the high-tech leader replied.

"It must be great having all this within a reasonable drive."

"It is. I moved here from Utah some years back and really love it," he answered.

Indiana Dan chimed in: "What brings you clean out here from Ohio?"

"I heard so much about the John Muir Trail, and after walking the Appalachian Trail, I wanted to try some western hiking and see what all the fuss is about."

This conversation led into inquiries about my Appalachian trek. The Scout leaders' interest was piqued when I told them I had written a book about my journey. Beth chimed in and told the guys about our depression awareness campaign and shared our Hike For Mike story. Dan was ready to retool his pack and hike along with us, even more so after hearing of our cause.

Dan reflected on his relationship with his wife, explaining that he had never been able to get her out for a backpacking trip.

"She said that I'm free to go hiking without her, and she doesn't mind," Dan said.

It hadn't really dawned on me that Beth was probably the only female within a day's hike of here. There were plenty of female hikers scattered along the John Muir Trail, and I personally know of at least a dozen female thru-hikers from my Appalachian Trail journey. But this was definitely a male bonding, father-son trip we had crashed. Beth's presence seemed to stir the men about their own spousal relationships when it came to hiking. I know that my mind is overtaken by thoughts of Beth when I'm hiking alone. Conveniently leaving out the part about how it had taken me four years to convince Beth to backpack with me, I proudly announced to the guys: "Yeah, it's pretty cool hiking with my wife." With a positive upswing in my intonation, I knew I just scored major brownie points with Beth, but I was sincere.

The sun was long set. We said good night to our friendly neighbors and beamed our flashlights in the direction of our campsite. We zipped into our tent and fell right to sleep.

Chapter 12
Marlboro Man

Red's Meadow, 58 miles from Happy Isles
August 1, 2003

O ne of the amazing things that makes hiking in the back-country so enjoyable to me is the interesting people I meet and the friendships I build. No other activity I know compares. Many people unfamiliar with the backcountry culture naively equate hiking to getting away from it all—especially people. But it turns out that you meet many others getting away from it all when you get away. They tend to be like-minded folks, so quite a culture exists in the woods.

How often on a vacation have you walked into a restaurant and eaten dinner, and then checked into a hotel room with the complete strangers that sat near you during your meal? In the woods, it's standard practice to cook and eat your meal while talking with total strangers and then later roll out your sleeping bags essentially in a communal bedroom. Of course, this act of trust sometimes leads to unpleasant discoveries about your neighbors, such as loud snoring and other bodily music. Still, the wilderness has a way of coaxing people from their stubborn, leathery shells. It's rare today for a complete stranger to holler from his porch and invite you into his house for coffee, but out in the woods, I'm often invited to sit by the campfires of complete strangers who offer me food and drink. The friendliness I have experienced in the backcountry is genuine, old-fashioned hospitality that often is squelched by the fast-paced, gotta-go American lifestyle. Our Boy Scout encounter turned out to be great trail fellowship.

Beth and I awoke to voices. The Boy Scouts were walking past our tent to and from the stream to fill their water containers. The weather had been dry all night. We crawled out of our tent, and without a word, we embarked on our morning dance of boiling water for coffee, eating granola bars, and breaking camp. We were robot-like in our routine after three nights on the trail. The comforting, familiar smell of pancakes sizzling in butter swirled up our noses and teased our appetites. The Scouts were equipped with plenty of hot meals—one of the advantages of hiking in a big group on a short trip is the ability to divvy up the groceries and prepare lip-smacking meals. Despite spending just one evening at the same camp with these guys, our goodbyes were like those said to good friends. There was picture-taking, address-exchanging, and encouragements of "Look me up if you're ever in town."

Beth and I managed to break camp and hit the trail by 8 a.m. The guidebook trail profile of that day's walk resembled a serrated knife. It featured continual but brief ups and downs, as opposed to the jagged profiles of the previous few days. We were heading in the direction of Mount Ritter and Banner Peak, both towering around 13,000 feet. The JMT skirts these peaks, so hikers get spectacular views without having to actually climb over them.

Hikers and horseback riders are not the only outdoor enthusiasts enjoying the spectacular scenery. Mount Ritter and Banner Peak are popular among climbers as well, and John Muir himself climbed Mount Ritter. Beth and I were content with the views from the trail and had no ambitions or energy to take a side trip to climb. Besides, we lacked the technical equipment that climbers use, such as rope, carabiner clips, climbing shoes, belays, and anchors. You need serious gear for climbing. Failing to take the right precautions could be fatal.

The hiking was easy all morning, although the sky threatened rain. Beth and I reached a lake in a marshy meadow overlooking Banner Peak and were awestruck. Banner Peak did more than stand tall. Its deep gray rock cut sharply upward as if it had ambitions of climbing to heaven, and it seemed to be succeeding. The mountain was frosted with large white snow patches and garnished at the base by pine trees. From where we stood, we could see the whole breathtaking scene reflected in the calm lake. The mountain peak shimmered in the calm water just inches from our feet. A mother and her son walked up as Beth and I stood taking it all in. We swapped cameras and took turns posing with the lake and mountain in the background. The mother and son had come from the direction we were headed. They promised we would see more great views as we continued on toward Thousand Island Lake, named for the patches of land scattered throughout it.

Beth and I wormed along the rocky trail, tripping occasionally as we gazed at the magnificent view off to the right.

We descended gradually to the outlet of Thousand Island Lake, which offered a different angle of Banner Peak and Mount Ritter. A middle-aged couple sat along the bank, absorbed in the view. We kept quiet to avoid spoiling their serenity. They eventually stood up, walked over to us, and introduced themselves. They were endurance runners who had parked at a trailhead several miles from the JMT and were out for a stroll. Both had trotted every inch of the JMT on previous adventures, but that day they were on a relaxing day hike. The woman recognized our "Hike For Mike" T-shirts. "I've visited your website. Good work!" she exclaimed.

Even in the woods, news travels fast. The woman was up-to-date with the local hiking and trail running culture. She told us about a young man who wanted to run the JMT and try to beat the record.

"What is the record?" I wondered.

"Four and a half days," the woman replied.

"Wow!"

"He plans to start any day," she said.

Beth and I were walking eight- and ten-hour increments each day, with three weeks set aside to trek the entire JMT. The notion that someone actually ran this trail in fewer than five days seemed unreal. Beth is a three-time marathoner, and I'm athletic myself, but running in mountain terrain like this would be a whole new beast.

We left the couple near Thousand Island Lake, where they split off on a side trail back to their car. We continued on in full view of the breathtaking Ritter and Banner profiles. The trail wound around the perimeters of several lakes, and we shot an entire roll of film as we took turns playing Ansel Adams. We traversed a log-railing footbridge—one of the few—

perched several feet above a gushing whitewater lake outlet. So far, the gray sky had refrained from dumping on us.

Our goal was to trek 18 miles from where we camped with the Scouts—our longest day yet—all the way to Red's Meadow, a mountain resort near but not on the JMT. A high-school friend of Beth's planned to drive in from San Francisco and meet us. Arranging to meet up with people along a journey such as this is difficult, to say the least. Things don't always go as planned. Anything can happen out in the backcountry, such as injuries, storms, getting lost, or, say, leaving your clothes at the beginning of the trail and having to go back for them.

We marched up and over a brief series of switchbacks toward Garnet Lake, and we saw a hiker descending. He was approaching more quickly than we were reaching him. He stopped on the trail at the turn of a switchback, smiling as we approached. I could tell he had been out there for a while. He had a trance-like daze in his eyes, the kind long-distance hikers get as they walk and get lost in their thoughts. He had all the telltale characteristics of a long-distance hiker: an unkempt, scraggly beard; cheekbones that pushed out with a look of weight loss; and a deep bronze tan on his arms, legs, and face, with brilliant white skin peeking from beneath his shirt sleeves and socks. He had some gray woven into his jet-black hair, and I figured he was in his late 40s.

"Where are you coming from?" I asked.

"Mexico," he said matter-of-factly.

"So you're doing the PCT?" I asked, meaning the Pacific Crest Trail.

"Yeah, that's the plan."

This guy had been on the trail for more than 800 miles.

He had walked through waterless stretches in the Mojave Desert and over the highest mountain range in the continental United States. I was impressed. He said goodbye after our brief chat and continued maneuvering down the narrow switchback with the brashness of a self-assured long-distance hiker. The John Muir Trail joins with the Pacific Crest Trail except for a few bits and pieces, and the JMT stretch of the PCT through the Sierra is considered the most rugged segment of the entire PCT. The PCT is the west's version of the Appalachian Trail, but with more miles, more solitude, and more altitude. The John Muir Trail section of the Pacific Crest Trail is the most remote and challenging of the entire 2,600-mile PCT. According to the Pacific Crest Trail Association, approximately 300 hikers attempt the PCT each year. Many of them throw in the towel in the Sierra. Some succumb to the rugged challenge, and others simply fall in love with the raw beauty of the mountains and lose the desire to walk any further.

We zigzagged up and down switchbacks as we skirted a series of lakes. The trail dipped down into thick stands of trees along the edge of Shadow Lake and climbed up again toward Rosalie Lake. I pulled out the satellite phone during one of our breaks and called in an update to our webmaster. She posted our update immediately. We remained below the canopy of thick pine and fir forest. The mosquitoes amassed themselves in a full-bore assault on us. We had dropped almost a thousand feet in elevation, and the temperature felt warm. During a rest, I pulled some DEET from my pack— the strongest bug repellent on the market—sprayed myself, and passed the bottle to Beth. But these insects didn't seem bothered by the repellent. They continued to swarm, especially when we stopped. They would buzz near our ears with that all-too-familiar, annoying hum, which was psychologically aggravating. It was as if they knew we were wearing the strongest repellent but that it wasn't going to keep them from trying to drink us dry. We didn't stop for very long, hoping our wind momentum would keep them at bay. Rain persisted throughout the day, a misty drizzle that diluted the DEET.

The trail remained fairly level as we checked off more miles. We were now walking in dense forest that reminded me of my Appalachian Trail journey. We came across a man lying beneath a canopy made from a tarp tied between two trees. A large log lay on the trail nearby with its bark skinned off and woodchips scattered everywhere. We could hear a rhythmic chopping sound that echoed through the forest, and we found the source as we rounded the bend. A trail crew of three was hard at work. One worker was digging a trough in the trail that was deep and round enough to hold a tree trunk the circumference of a car hubcap, while the other two were skinning the bark off two fallen trees at least 20 feet long. They were trail crew workers earning every dime of their pay. Beth and I stopped to admire their work, and we thanked them. One of the workers stopped to talk with us. He gave us a brief lowdown on what they were doing

"We're rerouting this whole section of trail to stop the erosion. When we're done, you won't even see our work. To increase the longevity of the logs, we're skinning the bark off before burying them beneath the trail, which will help support the foot and horse traffic."

"Thank you again. We really appreciate all your work!" I said. I meant every word.

We began a dramatic descent that would last more than

five miles. We stopped only once to put on our sandals for a creek ford. Beth complained that her feet hurt. It had been a long day of walking, and she was holding up well, considering this was the longest she had ever gone wearing a full backpack in her entire life. The last few miles of trail were laden with deep, beach-like sand, which made each step tiresome despite the gravity that carried us downhill.

Our hiking was almost over for the day. We were hiking high along the canyon wall above the middle fork of the San Joaquin River and the nearby Devil's Postpile, a geological display of basalt columns, naturally shaped in perfect polygonal and towering 60 feet above. Devil's Postpile is such a geologic wonder that it, along with the nearby 101-foot Rainbow Falls, is protected by the National Park Service. In 2002, as many as 152,000 tourists visited the area, according to the NPS. John Muir himself traversed much of this area during his early days as a sheepherder. All of this surrounded our destination, Red's Meadow Resort. We descended into the canyon, crossed on a footbridge over the San Joaquin River, and began looking for Red's Meadow.

We just wanted to drop our packs, fill our bellies with food, and relax. The drizzle persisted. Several unmarked trails intersected the path, and we were confused about which way to go. We were tired and just wanted to stop hiking. In addition to our growing hunger and weary feet, we had the added pressure of a timeline to meet Beth's friend Bob and his fiancée at Red's Meadow Resort. We were nearing the time we planned to meet, but we had told them we might be late.

Finally, after choosing a gravel path, we came upon a road that we hoped would take us up to the resort. Thank goodness it did. The road wound up a pine-forested hill. We could hear distant music and the mixed voices of children and adults. We reached a crest in the road and saw a horse barn, cabins, and a fifth-wheel camper. Dozens of non-hiking vacationers wearing jeans, cotton polo shirts, and sandals lounged in chairs and strolled about. A turnaround horseshoe drive veered off to the left. Two one-story wooden buildings sat facing each other in the turnaround. A sign on one building read "Red's Meadow General Store." Beth and I walked to the store. We dropped our packs and leaned them up against a tree between the two buildings, laying our poles on top of our packs.

We were in cowboy country. Beth and I stepped into the store to find out about food and camping. The store carried fishing tackle, camping supplies, and enough food to re-supply if we needed anything. This was a popular supply point for PCT and JMT thru-hikers. Hikers often mail supplies addressed to themselves but in care of Red's Meadow Resort, and the store will hold them. Tourists milled in the aisles. We stood near the checkout counter and waited until the woman behind the counter finished with a small line of customers before we would spring all of our questions on her. Just as we were about to barrage the woman with questions, the screen door banged open and in walked a man that looked as if he just walked off the set of a Western. A beige, wide-rimmed cowboy hat adorned his head, and the face underneath was a deep tan with a few days' worth of beard stubble, as if he had just returned from a ride over the mountains. He wore a long-sleeved, button-down, cowboy-style shirt and leather chaps that were dusty and worn. He had a buck knife strung on his belt. I felt as if we had stepped back in time and at any minute were going to be summoned to the corral for a

*July 29, 2003: Beth and me at the beginning
of our journey at Yosemite National Park*

July 29, 2003: The Half Dome in Yosemite rises above the trees.

*July 29, 2003: It's only our first day on the trail
and already we have our first bear encounter.*

*July 30, 2003: Another of Yosemite's wildlife,
a curious marmot gets close enough and eyes us carefully.*

August 1, 2003: Majestic Banner Peak.

*August 2, 2003: Virginia Lake, the gateway
to the Sierra backcountry.*

August 5, 2003: Our abundant food cache at Vermillion Valley.

*August 6, 2003: Beth surprised by the weight
from new provisions.*

August 6, 2003: My first trout, caught at Rosemarie Meadow.

*August 8, 2003: Beth and I stop for a spell
at the Muir Pass Hut.*

August 9, 2003: Here I am, passing through a grazing fence.

August 10, 2003:
We take in the breathtaking
scenery below Pinchot Pass.

August 10, 2003:
Crossing Woods Creek on the
Golden Gate swingbridge.

*August 12, 2003: Our camp at the foot
of Mt. Whitney, the final mountain.*

*August 13, 2003: We were here! Beth signs in at
the Mt. Whitney Summit shelter.*

August 13, 2003: Sunrise over Guitar Lake.

August 13, 2003:
The family celebrates the end of the journey at Whitney Portal.
(l to r) Beth's Mom, myself, Beth, Beth's Dad, and Aunt.

shootout. He grabbed a carton of cigarettes, stuck them under his arm, and stood in line to cash out.

Red's Meadow Resort has quite a history. Bob Tanner, the current owner, acquired the resort in 1960. The resort sits along an old wagon train route dating back to the gold-mining days. Folks would cross the Sierra from Mammoth Lakes, a valley town on the east side of the mountain, to Oakhurst in the western valley. In 1935, John Wayne filmed a movie using nearby Rainbow Falls as a backdrop. In 1972, Ronald Reagan—then governor of California—rode by horse up to the resort to declare formally that a proposed highway would not be built through the wilderness that surrounded the resort. Numerous celebrities have spent time at Red's Meadow Resort, including Tom Hanks, who has booked several horseback excursions out to the Mount Ritter and Banner Peak area. Bob Tanner has more than 100 horses, and he allows tourists to participate in his annual horse drive. Cowboys drive horses and mules up the mountain in the spring and back down to the valley in the fall, Old West style. Bob's horses have been seen in several Westerns, including *How the West Was Won, North To Alaska,* and *Nevada Smith.* This was more than a stop for the night off the trail—this was a Marlboro Man experience.

After the cowboy cashed out, I asked the store clerk what kind of lodging was available. She pulled out a map, showing us the campgrounds further down the road from where we were. Then she told us that a cabin unexpectedly became vacant and was available for the night. The cabin cost quite a bit more than Beth and I had expected to pay, and besides, we had all the necessary camping provisions. We looked outside at the rain smacking into deep puddles. I told Beth it was up to her. The next thing I knew, the woman behind the counter was writing us a receipt for a cabin and handing us a key.

"How late does the Mule Horse Café serve dinner?" I asked, referring to the restaurant in the building adjacent to the store.

"You both better get over there and order because they're closing right now."

Beth hurried over to the diner and ordered us dinner while I finished up with the room transaction. The restaurant was clean and cozy with a wood-burning stove in one corner, a snack bar, and pictures of celebrities that had visited Red's Meadows sprinkled all over the white walls. Beth ordered us both the special of the day, lasagna, which was delicious. The waitress poured us both coffee and delivered salads, which we consumed in a matter of minutes. She brought plates with heaping portions of lasagna oozing over the plate edges, and while we were eating, she returned to scrape the last of the lasagna pan onto our plates. She was used to hungry hikers stopping in for supper, and she knew how to make them happy. Even with our enormous appetites, we couldn't finish. We ended up boxing up the leftovers to bring to our cabin.

We keyed into our cabin, which was within a stone's throw of the restaurant, and we immediately removed our boots and found the shower. Beth went first. While she was in the shower, I heard a vehicle pull up and a door slam shut. I watched as a key turned and our cabin door swung open. A woman wearing a shocked expression stood staring at me in my underwear. I can't imagine what she was thinking as she encountered my unshaven, half-naked self standing inside what she presumed was her cabin. Behind her sat an idling, sparkling black Humvee, and her husband and kids were gathering their luggage and getting ready to make our cabin their home for the night. I felt bad as I explained to her that there must have been some mix-up because we already had booked the cabin and settled in.

"We can share the cabin if they don't have any more rooms, though," I offered.

"No, no, we'll find something," the woman replied as she backed off the porch. She must have caught a whiff of my socks hanging off my pack by the door. They had enough kick to scare a skunk away.

After we showered off the trail grime, we stepped out to see if Beth's friend Bob and his fiancée had made it. We found Bob wandering near the general store, looking for us. He explained that his fiancée had a schedule conflict and couldn't make it. We showed him to the cabin.

Beth had known Bob since high school. Beth said they always had been nothing more than good friends, so I didn't feel awkward that he had arrived without his fiancée, even though Bob had a pact with Beth that if neither of them was married in five years from their college graduation, they would marry each other. Bob surprised us with a bottle of California wine from the Sonoma vineyards. For the next several hours, we sat around the kitchen table, sipping some of California's finest red and sharing stories. Beth was catching up on who had gotten married, who was working where, and other trivia of her friends from her early years. All of Beth's friends had been tremendously supportive of her after she lost her brother—Bob included. He wanted to help out with our expedition anyway he could. Driving six hours to greet us with a bottle of excellent California wine in a remote wilderness area was beyond kindness. He helped remind us of the incredible support we enjoyed.

Morning came fast. Beth, Bob, and I wandered over to the Mule House Café for a hearty breakfast—again more food than our hearty appetites could handle. Bob brought some basic hiking equipment and insisted on spending a night in the backcountry with us. I reviewed a map with him and found a side trail off the JMT where he could drive to, park, and hike up to our planned camping spot. We could all camp together, and he could return to his car easily the next day. Bob would drive down to the resort town of Mammoth Lakes, leave his car in a campground near Mammoth Consolidated Mine, and walk up the mountain to meet us at the trail junction. Beth and I would leave from Red's Meadow on foot, continuing our southbound walk along the JMT.

After reviewing logistics one last time, Beth and I waved goodbye to Bob, slung on our packs, and ambled through the resort, passing the horse barn and snapping a few pictures of the cowboys who were more than eager to pose. We had descended quite a bit in elevation and were currently at 7,400 feet. It was August 2. We had been walking for five days and almost 60 miles. That day we would climb around 3,000 feet over a 12-mile stretch. As a rule of thumb, whenever you're within reach of domesticated amenities, you descend in elevation, and when you leave domestic amenities, you ascend the mountain. The sun was shining above us in a partly cloudy blue sky. Our spirits were lifted with the combination of Bob's visit and improving weather.

It's well documented that exposure to sunlight helps increase serotonin and improves your mood. That was one of the attractions that convinced Beth to walk the JMT with me. The JMT is known to have some of the sunniest mountain conditions in the world. This would not only keep our spirits high but would help us inform others of the healthy aspects of walking in the outdoors—that hiking benefits your body in more ways than the physical.

As we summited our first ridge, the trail leveled off briefly. We agreed to stop for a rest. We had been walking through a hillside of burnt forest. In 1992, a lightning strike sparked a forest fire that nearly wiped out Red's Meadow Resort. With the help of sand, water, manpower, and Mother Nature, the fire was diverted from the resort, but it burned whole hillsides of forest. Looking back the way we had trekked, we could see hundreds of acres of burnt forest with nothing but dead pine logs protruding from the grass-covered hillsides like the needles on the back of a porcupine. It was hard to imagine how hot and fierce this fire was to have caused so much damage. I'm sure a lot of wildlife perished. It's one thing to see these wildfires on the news, but to see the destruction in person is overwhelming.

We met up with Bob at our planned rendezvous without any problems, and we found a campsite in a small canyon overlooking the Silver Divide. We set up our tents under the shade of a small stand of trees. Bob surprised us again by pulling out a few cans of beer he had carried up the mountain. I felt like we were in a beer commercial as we enjoyed a few cold ones amid the mountain views and remote wilderness.

We sat around chewing on beef jerky and sipping brews. I wandered down to a nearby stream to pump-filter some drinking water and scoop some water into my pan to boil for dinner. Beth gave herself a towelette bath in our tent and put on her camp outfit. We selected a freeze-dried teriyaki chicken for our main course. We pulled out all the stops in

consideration of our guest and prepared some instant chocolate cheesecake for dessert—just add cold water and stir. As
soon as the sun set, the temperature dropped dramatically,
and a chilling wind sent us scurrying into our tent.

We woke up the next morning to a chilly 38 degrees. After
some hot coffee and breakfast energy bars, we said goodbye
to Bob. I handed him a roll of film that he agreed to develop
and e-mail to our webmaster, who would post the photos
to our website. We wanted those following along to get a
glimpse of what we were experiencing on the trail.

Chapter 13
Fishing 101

Purple Lake, 73 miles from Happy Isles
August 3, 2003

August 3 was the first full day of sunny blue sky of the trip. In fact, it marked the beginning of endless sunny weather for the rest of our expedition. The weather had been rainy and cold for the first five days of our journey, and we finally were blessed with a cloudless sky. With nothing but rich, daydreamy blue as far as we could see, this was the kind of JMT weather everyone boasted about. Also that day, my fishing license became valid. I would have free reign—in accordance with the rules of California Department of Fish and Game—to drop my fishing line in the lakes and streams all along the John Muir Trail for the rest of our journey. I had purchased a ten-day license in the outfitter store back in Yosemite Valley and postdated it for this date. I thought it would allow us time to adjust to trail life before attempting to fish, something I had never done while hiking. I honestly never thought the day would come when I would actually want to fish for pleasure.

In 1993, I had promised my dad a fishing trip for his birthday. To this day, I don't know what I was thinking. I am missing the successful fisherman gene. As a young boy, my family camped frequently at a nearby campground. My dad would take my brothers and me down to the stocked pond at the campground with our bamboo fishing poles in hand. These poles didn't have casters. The fishing line was tied to a loop hook at the end of the pole. We baited our hooks, swung our poles behind us, and whipped them forward, tossing our lines as far as we could from shore. And then we would wait for one of the starving, overstocked fish to bite our line and yank down our bobber. We were so excited as we pulled the fish to shore. Dad taught us how to remove the fish from the hook and place the fish in a bucket of water, which we would dump back into the pond when we were done.

On one of my casts, my fishing line never reached the water. My hook had snagged my brother Todd's ear. At first I thought I was stuck on some weeds, so I pulled hard, trying to break free. But Todd swung around toward me with a panicked look in his eyes, my hook pierced through his bloody ear. Todd and I marched back to our campsite with him leading and me following, as if I had caught him and was marching him through camp. Mom cut the line from my pole, and Todd was rushed to the hospital, where he received several stitches.

Over the years, I had lost all interest in fishing. I had nothing against it, really. It's just that hiking filled my outdoor needs just fine, and there weren't any hooks involved. Besides, I enjoyed being active outdoors, and I thought fishing was rather sedentary.

My dad loved to fish. So despite my lack of interest, I decided to put my preferences aside and try to do something nice for my dad for his birthday. We didn't own a boat, but we lived within a short drive of Lake Erie, which abounds in perch, walleye, and bass. The nearby truck-rental facility just so happened to rent fishing boats complete with little outboard engines. Of course, the people at the company wanted the whole world to know where the boat came from, so they painted a big company logo in don't-shoot-me colors on its side. Not only was it used to snag new customers, but it also branded Dad and me as inexperienced on the high seas.

We set aside a Saturday, assembled all of Dad's fishing tackle, drove out to Port Clinton—a small town on the shore of Lake Erie—and backed our little rental boat down the ramp and into the water. We threw our tackle in the boat, and we were off. Of course, neither of us really knew where to go. I commandeered the vessel away from shore, pivoting the little outboard motor by its handlebar-like steering mechanism and wondering where we should stop and drop our lines. We noticed groups of boats huddled together that were pulling in fish left and right. They had sonar. We followed them wherever they went.

These other boats also had experienced skippers and plenty of gas, two attributes we lacked aboard our vessel. We followed the boats farther and farther out to sea as they tracked a school of fish. In no time, we filled a five-gallon bucket with perch—enough for the two of us to live off for three or four days. We were now several miles off shore, and it was late in the day. Most of the other boats had wrapped up and were motoring in. We decided we'd had enough and should head in as well. Shortly after starting the boat and pointing it toward the shore, the engine hesitated, coughed its last breaths, and puttered out. After pulling the start cord a few times, I opened the gas tank, which was an empty, echoing chamber.

"I'll row us in, Dad. Don't worry. It will just take us a while longer," I blurted.

I splashed the oars into the water, but for every row I made, the lake seemed to produce a counteractive wave that pulled us twice as far out to sea. Dad sat facing me in the bow of the boat, wrapped in a bulky, brightly colored life vest. He clenched the boat sides with his hands, trying to stay calm. This was not your ordinary, run-of-the-mill landlocked lake. Lake Erie is a world shipping route with shipping lanes and the whole deal. Storms that brewed up out there had swallowed entire ocean freighters, and there we sat in an aluminum puddle jumper, drifting aimlessly out to sea. I rowed desperately.

"Jeff, we're just going further out to sea," Dad said.

"Well, what else can I do?" I snapped.

A large white yacht appeared on the horizon of the lake, heading in our general direction on its way to port. We both stood up and waved our hands frantically, hoping someone would see we needed help. The closer it got, the larger it looked. Luckily, someone on board spotted us. The yacht cruised within close range of us. A crewman tossed us a rope and instructed us to tie the rope to a loop hook protruding from the bow of our boat. Several folks stood on the deck of the yacht and laughed at our helpless, pathetic-looking selves bobbing in our minnow-size rental. We were getting knocked all around from the waves coming off their whale-size vessel. The whole way in to shore, we were both thankful and embarrassed as our boat trailed off the back end of the yacht.

We were safely inside its wake, but we were being bounced around enough to remind us how vulnerable we were to being swallowed up by the lake. Dad got more than a fishing trip—he got an adventure. This fishing episode, along with my childhood incident with my brother, was permanently etched in my mind. I had lost all ambitions of wanting to ever fish again.

So when I announced to my dad that I was going to try my luck with trout fishing along the JMT, he was pleasantly surprised. Many of the JMT journals I had read mentioned how abundant the trout were in the lakes and streams all through the Sierras. The key word and phrase mentioned in JMT trail journals that convinced me to try trout fishing were "novice" and "If I can catch fish, anyone can." A hiking friend who had walked most of the JMT during his Pacific Crest Trail journey told endless stories of how he easily caught dinner all through the Sierra using just fishing line and spinners. Many hikers boasted of being able to supplement their diets with protein from trout all along the trail. I thought fishing along the trail would help with my chest-beating, nomadically romantic notion of Beth's and my journey together. Man catch fish, provide food for woman, grrrr!

A sponsor had given me a collapsible, lightweight traveler's rod and reel. My brother-in-law, who is quite the fisherman, brushed me up on cleaning and preparing the fish to fry. My dad, excited that I was going to give fishing another shot, gave me a little pocket-sized fishing guidebook. My brother Larry gave me a few lures, showed me how to secure them to a hook on my fish line, and suggested that I check with the locals about what they have found successful. Even with all the helpful advice and equipment, I was still wary of my ability and carried plenty of food so that we wouldn't have to rely on my luck at fishing to maintain our strength.

A few miles after leaving camp and saying goodbye to Bob, we walked up and over a brief incline and descended down along the north shore of Purple Lake—at 9,900 feet—which looked more black than purple. Temperatures had warmed quite a bit from the 38 degrees we awoke to. Beth and I shed our jackets down to our T-shirts and long hiking pants, with the bottoms still zipped onto our shorts.

"Beth, do you mind if I stop and try fishing here?"

"That's fine," she answered, knowing how excited I was to try my luck.

This first attempt would prove unsuccessful. After extending my telescoping rod—an action I had craved since starting our journey—and clipping my fly onto my pole, I spent quite a bit of time figuring out how to cast. For more than an hour, I continually threw my line out into the water as far as I could and slowly reeled it in, hoping a trout would mistake my lure for an actual bug. No chance. Beth sat along the shoreline on a rock, reading a book she had pulled from her pack. I didn't even try to pretend to know what I was doing in front of Beth. She had heard all the stories and knew I couldn't fish. She also knew that my failed efforts would be due to operator error and not for lack of fish. We could see the buggers swimming inches from shore, surely laughing at my inadequate technique. Occasional ripples on the water's surface as the trout nabbed real insects underscored the fact that they weren't fooled by my lure. Several species of trout live in the Sierra—brook, brown, golden, and rainbow—and all of them thrive in the glacially cold lakes and streams. After about an hour of effort, I gave up.

This was the first time we had stopped along the trail to do nothing but relax. We usually only stopped for a rest, a snack, a bathroom break, or to set up camp. So from one perspective, it was a pleasant experience. We had been so focused on making time to meet Bob earlier that we now could slow up a bit. It's amazing how weather and a visit from a friend can change the whole day. We didn't have to wear parkas because no rain threatened us; we didn't have to worry about lightning, and our moods were upbeat and happy.

I strapped my fishing rod back to my pack, and we climbed up from Purple Lake along a ridge and then descended down to what Beth has declared the most beautiful lake she has ever seen: Lake Virginia. This was as close as she would get to her preferred beach vacation, minus the piña coladas, Jimmy Buffet music, and endless sunbathing. Actually, about the only two commonalities between this trip and a day at the beach were a body of water and the fact that we were slathered in sunscreen.

As we followed the trail down to the lake, Beth's eyes were zombie-like. She was lost in thought as she looked out across the sparkling blue water. On the far side of the lake stood scattered pines and snow-patched mountains. We stood on a grassy shoreline that was studded with bleached white rocks the size of beach balls. The blue sky iced the view, tempting us to set up camp and stay. But it was only noon, and we had walked only a little more than six miles. We still had at least eight hours of daylight left.

Beth said she was thinking of Mike a lot and wishing he could be with us, but that this place made her feel a lot better. Before we moved on, I pulled her close for one of my famous one-handed camera shots, for which I hold the camera out in front of the both of us with one hand, aim it as well as I can without actually being able to see the background, and snap a picture.

We were within a day's hike of our planned re-supply point. The trail skirted Lake Virginia, allowing Beth to continue in her zone of thought as we walked. We forded a stream and then descended dramatically back and forth along the edge of a tree-speckled mountainside to a canyon named Tully Hole. A mountain stream ran through it. We climbed out of Tully Hole and eventually reached the highest point of our day: Silver Pass at 10,900 feet. With the sun shining down from a cloudless sky onto a treeless landscape, we realized the importance of wearing sunscreen. Despite the brisk, chilly winds, it was hot out. Our arms were turning a deep red through the sunscreen we had caked on. We were using large, lip-balm-looking sunscreen sticks that claimed to be waterproof and protect us with SPF 30.

We descended from Silver Pass, skirting two lakes. A man and a boy passed us in the other direction toward their camp. The boy was carrying a ring of trout—one longer than ten inches—they had pulled out of a nearby lake.

Toward the end of the day, we dramatically descended almost 3,000 feet. *The Guide to the John Muir Trail* had been very reliable for trail information. The authors mentioned that we would cross a few dangerous streams on the descent from Silver Pass and specifically stated, "a fall in one of these streams could be fatal." I appreciated being informed of any upcoming dangers, especially when it comes to the possibility of drowning. The guidebook authors must have passed through this section in the early season. I had read numerous trail journals and spoken with several park rangers about the dangers of stream fords along the JMT. Almost everyone agreed that the best way to avoid dangerous high water was to wait until late July or early August to hike. The Sierra are covered in snow most of the year, and the summer hiking season is limited. During the first part of July, snowmelt increases the water levels in the streams and covers many of the rocks that Beth and I were now fortunate enough to hop across easily. We specifically planned the timing of our hike around this very issue. Hiking to me is relaxing and rejuvenating, so I try to keep my hikes safe.

Beth and I received assurances from a hiker coming from the opposite direction that the crossings up ahead weren't bad—just a little wet. We both crossed without any difficulties other than wet feet. Our confidence rose. We knew we were past two of the JMT's most notorious river fords.

After steeply descending Silver Pass, Beth and I walked along a relatively flat section of trail with hikers' tents strung out all along a tranquil mountain stream. We found a secluded campsite nestled along the stream, out of sight but within shouting distance of other hikers. After setting up camp and eating dinner, I tried fishing with no success. I hoped my luck would improve.

Chapter 14
The Cheeseburger Cache

Vermilion Valley Resort, 90 miles from Happy Isles
August 4, 2003

Beth and I were strategically camped a short distance from our planned re-supply point, Vermilion Valley Resort. The farther we traveled from Yosemite—the beginning of our expedition—the more we distanced ourselves from civilization. We also were climbing in elevation, which meant less oxygen to breathe and more rugged terrain with each mountain pass. During the first half of our trip, we seemed to encounter some sort of domesticated amenity every few days. But Vermilion Valley Resort marked our last opportunity to buy a Coke, take a shower, and spend money.

That morning, we broke camp and walked along a relatively flat trail shaded by forest to the shoreline of Lake Edison, named after the inventor of the light bulb, Thomas Edison. Appropriately, Lake Edison is part of a hydroelectric dam system. The shoreline we stood along had once been the side of a mountain, which likely offered a commanding view of the now-flooded valley that Lake Edison filled. The area once was also inhabited by Mono Indians, some of whom still live throughout the area.

Vermilion Valley Resort was five miles off the John Muir Trail by a side trail: Mono Creek Trail, which ran along the lake edge. For a fee, Vermilion Valley Resort offered a ferry-boat shuttle across the lake to the resort. We had planned our arrival at the shore in time to catch the morning ferry, but at the last minute we decided to walk the lakeshore and save the $16 it would cost us for the one-way boat ride. Besides, it was a beautiful day, and we were planning to take a few days off at the resort.

The ferry reminded Beth of a family vacation to Washington state during her childhood. To save a few bucks, her dad and uncle told the kids to huddle underneath blankets in the back of her uncle's pick-up truck so they wouldn't have to pay the ferry cost for each child. Mike told their Aunt Pat what was going on, and she'd made the men apologize and pay the full price to the ferry service.

The trail around the lake was more than we bargained for. Looking at the map, we assumed the trail would be a relatively flat, serene beachside stroll. We were wrong. The trail wound up and down hills as if we were on a never-ending roller coaster erected in the forest. It dawned on me as we toiled along that because this wasn't a natural lake, we weren't walking along a natural path. Instead, we were traversing ripples of mountaintops. A manmade trail had been carved out to allow for foot travel. We arrived at Vermilion Valley Resort—exhausted—several hours after regretfully declining the ferry ride. We definitely got more than $16 worth of hiking.

While planning our trip, I had read numerous journals

of hikers who raved about their stays at this resort. I had reserved a private room, but we were a day ahead of our planned arrival and hoped to bump up our room reservation. One of the selling points to convince Beth that she would enjoy this journey was that we would be staying at a resort halfway through our hike—complete with private room, good food, drinks, and a lake view. What she was about to find out was that this was resort living by hiker standards. There would be no massage therapist, maid service, hot tubs, or chocolates on the pillows. In the backcountry, food and beer service qualifies a place as a "resort." We emerged from the forest and spotted a bark-brown, metal-roofed building. A sign on the wall next to the front entrance read: "Canada 1767 – Mexico 871," meaning the miles from each destination via the Pacific Crest Trail. A gas engine generator buzzed away annoyingly, but our thoughts were redirected when the smell of food hit us.

Beth and I set down our trekking poles, dropped our packs, leaned them against a nearby tree, and stepped inside. Just inside the door, we found a small, cluttered, two-aisle store with a glass display counter chock full of fishing lures and supplies. The two narrow aisles were packed with assorted hiking and camping supplies, and a cooler at the end of the aisles was stocked with milk, beer, soda, and sports drinks. An adjacent doorway led into a small café with a few booths lining the walls and tables and chairs arranged in the center of the room. An old iron wood-burning stove stuck out from the wall. Atop it, a metal cowboy coffee pot right out of a John Wayne movie emitted a powerful aroma from its spout, promising enough caffeine to wake the weariest of hikers. Along the back of the room was a rectangular window cut out of the wall that separated the small dining room from a galley-style kitchen. The window ledge was full of plates stacked with steaming food waiting to be delivered to tables, and two men were flipping burgers, stirring casseroles, and buttering toast to keep up with hungry hiker demands. This was one of the most notable stop-offs along the John Muir and Pacific Crest trails. An establishment earns popularity among hikers when it delivers both quantity and quality in the food department.

A double-paned sliding door next to the wood-burning stove led out to a rustic, canopy-covered patio, where a handful of hikers gathered. The patio perimeter was lined with a thick log counter held up with log legs. Tree stumps placed on both sides of the bar served as stools. Deep pine forest encroached on this bustling little lakefront outpost. An attractive, college-age woman emerged from the building to deliver hot plates of food to some nearby hikers, who were sipping beers as they waited. After walking in such rugged country, this was a surreal sight. We saddled two log barstools, and our eyes bulged as we watched the hot food being delivered.

"The first beer is on us. What would you like?" the waitress inquired. I had read about the free-beer tradition for hikers, and now we were experiencing it. Minutes later, two beers were placed before us in frost-covered mugs. Man, did those first few sips taste good. We ordered cheeseburgers and fries, which everyone recommended. The burgers hit the spot. While we sat eating, the cook emerged onto the pavilion and sat down for a break. He had a pleasant, sociable manner that made us want to get to know him. Intellectual words peppered his conversation, and that raised our curiosity even more. We learned that he was a retired Berkeley professor.

He'd hoped to find something eclectic and different to do, so he answered a want ad for a cook at a remote mountain resort. He was not a hiker by any means, so I imagined he was getting some new experience.

The trail culture was more solitary out here than on the Appalachian Trail. When I walked the AT, I stayed in or near three-walled shanties each night, mingling with other hikers as we walked into towns to re-supply. Each shelter had a notebook register for hikers to leave notes for those who followed. Trail camaraderie was a big part of the AT experience. Until now, our John Muir Trail journey was far less social than my AT adventure. Shelters were non-existent, which meant hikers stayed in tents or slept secluded under the stars. There were no trail journals to use to communicate. We had been socializing with hikers we passed along the way, but other than our one night with the Boy Scouts, our camp usually was quite a distance from anyone else's. Our visit to Vermilion Valley Resort was an intimate social gathering compared to what our trail encounters had been.

A group of hikers stood around a picnic table behind us. Piles of food covered every inch of table. This was a guided group of six hikers who had paid a decent amount of money to walk the John Muir Trail. The guide was doing all their logistical planning, preparing meals, arranging for supplies to be delivered along the trail by horse and mule, mapping, and keeping up morale. For the most part, the paying hikers just needed to focus on walking. Even with the luxury of being free of logistical stresses, one of the hikers had decided to quit right there at Vermilion Valley, almost halfway through the trip. The hike just wasn't for him. The terrain would only get more difficult as the group climbed higher in elevation and further from civilization.

After eating, we stepped into the store to see about bumping up our reservation. No chance. The rooms were full. No refunds, either. The clerk advised us that we could camp for free in the hiker tent cabin—a square, canvas-walled hut with military-style bunks—or we could assemble our tent nearby. The cabin was full, so we erected our tent. For $5, we were issued towels and the opportunity to shower in a mildewed, closet-size stall. Old, dust-covered campers and RVs sprinkled the shaded resort grounds. Pavilion roofs were built over them, so it was obvious that they hadn't been moved in quite some time. The resort staff lived in them.

Beth and I had planned to send an e-mail newsletter update to our sponsors and everyone following our journey on the "Hike For Mike" website when we reached Vermilion Valley Resort. The camp store clerk charged us by the minute to use its generator-powered desktop computer. We had been calling in updates to our webmaster every few days, and she was posting them on our website. Beth and I assembled an outline of the highlights of our journey, explaining the terrain and our expectations for the coming days. We took turns dictating and typing. In no time, we had assembled our official newsletter from the trail. Our webmaster cleaned it up a bit and forwarded the letter to all who had subscribed to receive it. It was inspiring to know that we had hundreds of people rooting for us from all over the country—Alabama, California, Florida, Illinois, New York, Michigan, Ohio, and Virginia, to name a few. We even had supporters in England.

Beth and I decided to get all of our chores done that day so we could relax without worries the next day when we moved into our room. Our only chore the next day would be to sort through the supply box we had mailed to ourselves at the resort. But first on our list was laundry. Two washers sat back to back against two dryers beneath a small pavilion roof in the center of the compound. Dingy, discolored T-shirts, socks, and shorts sat piled in mounds atop each washer as hikers waited their turns. We were in line behind a tall, lanky man with a British accent and a shiny bald head. He was one of the guided hikers—a businessman from San Diego—and he said he was enjoying his adventure.

Many of the hikers had gathered like hobos around a fire burning inside an old steel truck rim in front of the tent cabin. They were unshaven and unwashed, but their top-of-the-line gear and clothing guaranteed they weren't hobos. They were PhDs, actors, teachers, lawyers, business elites, and college students. As the dinner hour rolled around, the social circle worked its way to the restaurant for a massive feast and then returned to the fire. Beth and I shared in a few spirited beverages while getting to know some of the hikers.

We met a young aspiring actor who had walked the JMT several times. He noticed our "Hike For Mike" shirts and showed us his weirdly coincidental "Swim With Mike" shirt. He was involved with an event that raised money for kids with leukemia. He posed for a picture with Beth, each wearing a respective Mike shirt. We met a middle-aged couple—schoolteachers from Oregon—taking advantage of their summer off. There were five co-ed hikers from the same college who were more preoccupied with beer drinking than socializing. We met two attractive professional women walking together, several professors and post-doctoral students, and a retired couple from Toronto. The evening ferry shuttled some of the hikers back to the trail to continue their journeys and brought more new faces for us to meet.

At 10 p.m., the entire camp fell silent and dark with the throw of the generator switch. The annoying hum we had all grown used to fell silent. We retreated to our tent and fell soundly to sleep. Around sunrise, the generator fired up, awaking us. The morning was a cool 40 degrees. The smell of bacon drew us to the main pavilion. We looked forward to sipping some hot coffee and eating a hearty breakfast prepared by someone else. The small dining room was stuffed full of hikers who would depart on the morning ferry after breakfast.

Beth and I walked down to the beach lakefront to wish everyone farewell as they boarded the official ferryboat, an aging pontoon vessel. We had known these hikers for less than 24 hours, but it seemed like a lifetime. Outside observers watching us say goodbye might conclude that we all were relatives. We had a common bond: walking the John Muir Trail. Even if we didn't see another person for the rest of our journeys, it was fulfilling enough to know some of the others who were out there on the same mission as we.

The night before, several hikers had seen our "Hike For Mike" shirts and asked who Mike was. Beth shared the special reason behind our journey, tearing up as she explained that her brother Mike had taken his own life. Several hikers shared personal stories of people they knew who had depression or who had committed suicide.

We picked up our food cache from the store and checked into our room. Our room was dilapidated. Rust-colored rings on the ceiling told of years of water leaks; warped, scuffed 1960s paneling peeled at the seams on the walls; the sagging bed looked as if a boulder had dropped into the center and formed a permanent crater. There was no TV, radio, or telephone. As a matter of fact, the only phone at this resort was the owner's cell phone, which he allowed limited use of for $1 a minute. The room had a mini refrigerator, a small table, and two chairs. I kept my disappointment to myself. I had promised Beth a romantic night in a luxurious room, and this room surely would be condemnable by most city standards. But even though the bed linens were dingy, they were clean. The good food, nice conversation, and friendly staff made up for the room's shortfalls. Needless to say, we spent the entire day outside our dreary room.

We dumped our box of supplies onto a picnic table outside and began sorting and separating into his and hers piles. When we mailed our cache a week before beginning our trek, we hadn't anticipated cramming our food into the bear canisters. There was no physical way that we would be able to fit all our new food supplies in these canisters. We made some decisions we would later regret—discarding some bagels and ramen noodles, and eating our summer sausage and cheese block for lunch. We would learn later that we needed every crumb of food we were discarding. Beth's appetite was increasing to amounts comparable to my food portions—something I hadn't anticipated.

We stomped, pounded, and pressed as much food as we could into our bear canisters, then we put re-supplying aside. I walked up to the store and talked with one of the employees about fishing. He sold me a couple of spinners that were popular for trout in the Sierras. He gave me some basic pointers for dropping my line in some of the deeper areas of the streams and slowly reeling my spinner. The motion would simulate a bug. I practiced casting and reeling in the lake while Beth sat on a nearby rock to read.

The day slipped by. After eating dinner, we retreated to our room. The power went out at 10 p.m., but our room had an oil lamp and heater. In the morning, we awoke to the familiar generator buzz. We climbed out of the center pit of the mattress and marched up to the diner for a hot breakfast. The positive result of staying the night in a dumpy room was that we looked forward to sleeping in our tent once again.

We lugged our heavily fortified backpacks down to the lake and boarded the pontoon along with a dozen other folks for the ride across the lake. Some of the passengers were heading out for a day hike and planned to return on the evening shuttle. Some were along for the round-trip lake excursion. One passenger was a freelance photographer with two bulky cameras hanging off her neck. The captain of the vessel had the motor cover removed and was tinkering with the engine. It wouldn't turn over. I sat there wondering if we would have to walk the trail around the lake back to the John Muir Trail. Long-distance hikers try to avoid logging too many miles off the beaten path—they're considered pointless miles. After 30 minutes of troubleshooting, we abandoned ship into two small aluminum boats with outboard motors. Beth and I sat in the rear of our boat near the young captain, John. He pointed out a peregrine nest along the shore and explained how the Mono Indians traded goods along Mono Creek before it was flooded to make the lake. John explained that the resort was closed in the winter except for the occasional ice-fishing group that came in by helicopter. John's wife was the young waitress who had served us our complimentary beer and breakfast each day at the resort.

John told us how they tried to purchase the resort recently

after the original owner took his own life. Beth and I stared at each other. The owner had taken his own life. Even out here among all this natural beauty, in this seemingly stress-free environment, suicide was present.

Our ride came to an end as we reached the shore near the footpath that we would follow for the rest of our journey. We saddled ourselves with our packs, said goodbye to our captain and the other passengers, and headed down the trail.

Chapter 15
No Horsing Around

McClure Meadow, 119 miles from Happy Isles
August 7, 2003

This was it. We would not encounter any domestic amenities until we reached the end of our journey. What we had in our packs was all we would have to get us to Mount Whitney. We were energized from our brief break from hiking, but our packs were noticeably heavier with provisions. Our stay at Vermilion Valley Resort was below 8,000 feet. We hoped that the two days of R&R below altitude hadn't de-conditioned us to higher elevations. The sky was sunny and strikingly blue.

The trail was shaded by pine forest that provided us cover from the intense sun. We trekked a short distance from the lake along Mono Creek Trail, which soon connected with the junction where we had left the John Muir Trail. Shortly after turning south onto the JMT, we began a sharp back-and-forth ascent to the summit of Bear Ridge. The climb was more than 2,000 feet. We teetered as we walked, balancing our fresh provisions as we slowly progressed. It was as if we were roller coaster cars rolling up a tall hill without the comforting sound of chain links catching us and with heavy weights working against our momentum.

We had exited the boat around 11 a.m., which left us with a shortened day. We descended Bear Ridge, forded a few minor streams, and climbed once again for a short stretch as a stunning piece of landscape came into view. It was Rosemarie Meadow.

"We must stay the night!" I exclaimed.

My mom's name is Rose Mary, and I felt there must be some connection. We had walked a little more than ten miles, a respectable distance for a half-day of hiking in rugged country. We were once again at the elevation where altitude is a concern and the air is thin.

Our campsite had a romantic feel. We found a flat spot to set up our tent. It was surrounded by boulders and near a stream, with awesome views in every direction. The sky was a deep, cloudless blue. A creek slithered through the stands of pine trees with soothing miniature waterfalls. Boulders were strewn about, and distant mountains towered in every direction. A large granite mountain climbed above the trees to the south. We had stopped just shy of ascending Selden Pass. We had neither the daylight nor the energy for it.

We cooked and ate dinner before I tried my luck at fishing again. By now, I knew better than to hold off on supper. I stepped out onto some rocks in the stream nearby and cast my line into the water. On my third cast, something pulled down my line, and then it pulled harder. I reeled it in, mesmerized by the fish dangling from my hook. It was so small—five inches—that I threw it back, but not before posing for a few pictures. I had caught my first fish of the expedition. Something was working because in the next half hour, I reeled in five fish. All were smaller than six inches, so I threw them all back. Still, my confidence swelled. I knew I could catch fish out there. There was no size limit to these fish, only a number limit. Yee ha! We had an alternative food source. As the sun set, it cast rays onto the distant mountains, tinting them red and orange. It was alpenglow, and Beth and I sat on a rock as if we were watching fireworks.

We awoke to see our breath steaming in the cold morning air. Moisture beads dripped from the tent ceiling. Neither of us wanted to leave the warmth of a goose-down sleeping bag. Eventually, I climbed out of our frost-covered tent and put water on the stove for coffee. The thermostat hanging from my backpack zipper read 32 degrees.

By 7:30 a.m., we had packed up and began walking down the trail in fleece hats and gloves. The weather warmed quickly with the rising sun. Shortly after leaving camp, we ascended above the tree line. The trail wandered alongside Marie Lake, a glacial lake filled with deep blue water. By 10:30, we summited Selden Pass at 10,900 feet. We had bird's-eye views of the blue sky, lake, and granite rock speckled with greenery from the grass and trees far below. We had removed our jackets, gloves, and hats. We ran into two young men at the summit who took our picture, and then we descended Selden Pass, dramatically dropping almost 3,000 feet.

By midday, it warmed to 85 degrees. We quickly dropped beneath forest canopy and crossed a few small streams. I noticed flies swarming around my face and arms. They looked like houseflies, but they would land and bite. When they did, it stung like a bee sting and itched like a mosquito bite all in one shot. New England is notorious for its brief black fly season in the spring, but I never really thought about them being out here. I applied DEET to Beth and myself, but the flies didn't seem to mind. When we were out in the open wind, the flies didn't bother us, but when the air was still and we were in the trees, the flies swarmed. This went on all afternoon.

We caught up to Angie and Teresa, two women we had met back at Vermilion Valley. They were perched on a rock just off the steep switch-back trail and were sharing a large bag of potato chips. They had left Vermilion Valley a day before us.

"You two must be covering big miles," Angie said.

"We've been averaging 16 miles a day," I replied.

They had arranged food re-supplies every three days, which required leaving the JMT on descending side trails and hiking miles to reach access roads. Still, it allowed them to pack light and carry half the food Beth and I lugged in our bear canisters. Every technique has pros and cons.

The women said they had spent the previous night with Jim, an actor we had met back at the resort. Jim hiked ahead to pick up his supply box at Muir Trail Ranch—the only other halfway re-supply option for JMT hikers near the trail. We wished the women all the best on their journey and continued zigzagging back and forth down the mountain. We dropped into a canyon that was sandwiched between two mountains.

We stopped for lunch when we reached the bottom. As we fumbled through our packs for food, I heard something moving around in the trees. We both froze and focused our eyes in the direction of the sound. A grouse—a chicken-like bird that lives on the ground in the forest—came out onto the trail and paced in circles. During mating season, male grouse develop special air sacs on their necks to make a sound similar to a distant helicopter, which explains why I kept hearing helicopters. It's supposed to attract females. Some of the trees nearby were enormous. I stood for a picture between two ponderosa pines that were as big around as semi-truck tires.

The trail bottomed out. We walked along a relatively flat canyon and into Kings Canyon National Park, another milestone of our journey. Several hikers and fisherman were scattered about strategically beneath the shade of trees. We dropped our packs for a break, and I stepped down along the stream to pump-filter some water to replenish our empty water bladders. The temperature had reached nearly 90 degrees, and we had been in the open sun for the last several hours. The air was so dry that we could taste the dust we were kicking up.

We headed south on the trail, which soon emerged alongside the San Joaquin River. A treeless rock mountain jutted up on the other side of the river, making it obvious that we were in a canyon. Several folks in cowboy hats passed us on horseback in the opposite direction. The riders were on a guided scenic ride from Muir Trail Ranch several miles back. The canyon, the riders, and the trail snaking alongside the river conjured up images of Westerns. It seemed that at any moment, a rifle shot would echo through the canyon and John Wayne would gallop by, picking off bad guys high on the ridge above. Instead, we heard nothing but the rhythmic clank of our hiking poles as they poked into the dry, rocky trail with each step.

We continued our canyon river walk and came to a junction with a Goddard Canyon trail called Hell for Sure Pass. We were thankful that the JMT didn't route us along the Hell for Sure Pass trail, which I'm sure got its name from someone's miserable experience. Turning into Evolution Valley, we were approaching the most notorious river ford of the entire John Muir Trail. Beth and I had read several journals of hikers having hair-raising hardships crossing Evolution Creek. After a brief ascent up from the trail junction, we began to follow along the infamous creek, which boasted numerous cascading waterfalls and splashing whitewater. Our anxiety increased.

The dinner hour was approaching when the trail turned toward a wide-mouthed stream. It vanished at the water's edge and picked up again 30 yards across on the opposite bank. We hadn't had rain in more than a week, which was one thing in our favor. I walked along the creek's edge and debated whether we should cross at the trail junction or not. We decided that the current seemed less intense where the trail crossed. We removed our boots, tied them to our packs, and strapped on our sandals. We remounted our packs but left the hip belts and upper sternum straps undone in case we lost balance and had to slip out of the packs. Just as we were about to cross, a cowboy rode up. A pack mule loaded down with supplies was roped to his horse. The rider sat and watched us.

I decided to cross first so that I could make sure it was safe for Beth. I stepped into the cold water, which came up to my thighs at the deepest point and dampened my shorts the farther I got from shore. The swift current tried to sweep my hiking poles from my hands. I paused after each step and spiked a hiking pole down into the water in front of me before taking the next step. The rocks on the creek bottom were slippery. The opposite shore grew closer, my steps grew easier, and I finally made it to the other side. I dropped my pack and encouraged Beth.

"It wasn't that bad. You can do it!" I shouted. "Remember to place your pole ahead of you before taking a step."

I was sure she would be fine, but I was still nervous. She left the safety of shore and walked toward me. I grabbed my camera and took an action shot as Beth slowly navigated across.

"Good job, Beth!" I praised as she stepped up onto the bank.

The cowboy rode his horse into the creek, pulling the pack mule, as soon as Beth finished. When he reached our bank, he stopped on shore.

"You two are lucky. This creek was waist-deep just a few days ago," he said.

"Where are you going with the supplies?" I asked.

"To the ranger station at McClure Meadow," he replied.

I decided to take advantage of the possibility that he might be able to help us. If he took our trash, we'd have much more room in our cram-packed bear canisters.

"Could you pack out our trash?" I asked.

"Sure! Catch me in the morning up at the ranger station, and I'll pack it out for ya," he replied kindly.

We put our boots back on and followed the trail paralleling Evolution Creek.

We walked on to McClure Meadow, a popular camping spot. We were tired and hungry. Tents and hikers were scattered up and down the river's edge. We assembled our tent behind a car-size boulder for privacy from the other camps but within view of the creek. We had walked 20 miles, entered the second of three national parks on the JMT, and safely forded one of the most difficult stream crossings of the entire trek. What a day. We cooked up a freeze-dried Thai chicken dinner, removed our trail clothes, brushed our teeth, and planned to zip into the tent for the night. But the setting sun was again creating the alpenglow effect, which was too pretty to miss. I grabbed my camera and perched out on a rock along the creek, just in time to photograph a gray mountain across the creek turning a brilliant bold orange, then yellow, then back to granite again. All of these colors were reflecting off the creek water as I snapped pictures. It was mesmerizing every time. I wandered back to our tent and zipped us in for the night.

We both fell right to sleep and didn't wake up until Beth had to pee at 6 a.m. She unzipped our tent, slipped on her sandals, and dashed out into the cold morning air in a T-shirt and shorts. She hadn't been gone more than a minute when I heard the sound of a horse ride up and stop. A few moments later, I heard the horse trotting away. The sound became fainter and fainter, and then Beth crashed back into the tent with her sandals on and her color high.

"The cowboy just saw me going to the bathroom!" she announced.

Beth hadn't quite mastered the art of concealing herself when she relieved herself in the woods. She chose a spot along the trail, which at 6 a.m. should have been fine because all the other hikers were still asleep. But the cowboy's day started early. He was already in the saddle on his way out of the backcountry. Apparently, he recognized Beth, but when he got close he realized what she was doing. He didn't say a word—obviously embarrassed—but just sat there for a moment as if he were wondering what to do. He apparently wanted to live up to his promise of carrying out our trash. Beth—embarrassed as well—didn't speak a word and just kept on urinating as she stared back at the man. Even the horse seemed embarrassed. Beth didn't respond, so the cowboy probably began to feel like a voyeur and galloped off.

"Why didn't you tell him to wait a minute?" I asked.

"I'm not used to cowboys riding into my bathroom," she said.

Chapter 16
Take the Pain

Descent from Muir Pass, 130 miles from Happy Isles
August 8, 2003

We had our first spat on the trail. I don't know if it was the adrenaline rush that Beth was experiencing from the embarrassment of the cowboy incident or a sort of claustrophobia from our having been living in such close quarters. We had packed up camp and set out. When we stopped at the McClure Meadow ranger station, we met a real lone ranger, who lived a reclusive life several months a year. All his provisions were packed in by mule. He slept in a small cabin and relied on a solar-powered generator to run his park radio, which he used to communicate any emergencies and to check in every so often with the outside world. He walked his assigned territory every few days to make sure that the trail was intact, that hikers were O.K., and that the animals were performing all their park-service-assigned tasks—just kidding. A writer could get a lot done if he had this guy's job out here alone, as long as he could plug in a laptop, I thought as we set off.

For some reason, Beth and I were on edge as we walked away from the ranger station. I don't remember exactly who brought up what—heated emotions tend to distort facts—but we began to argue and stew over our popular hot topics of money, family, and food. Well, food was a constant topic on our minds out there. The argument grew more intense, and our voices grew louder. It was all right to yell—who would hear us? As I loudly disagreed with one of Beth's comments, two men rounded a bend ahead of us on the trail. The grins on their faces told us that they heard our last few volleys. We both forced fake smiles and greeted the men as they passed. We were embarrassed because we knew that they heard our ridiculous argument, but we were still settling scores. As soon as we were out of earshot, we got back into it. Whenever we had a disagreement back home, one of us usually left the other alone. This technique was next to impossible to pull off in the woods. I tried to hike faster than Beth to give us some time apart to cool off. Beth, feeling vulnerable to hungry mountain lions, wanted no distance between us and kicked in her athletic abilities to stay on my heels. I pushed myself harder, trying to pull away, but Beth remained close behind.

"Are you trying to ditch me?" she shouted.

I didn't respond. I was out of breath and still boiling from our disagreement. I also realized that Beth's hiking endurance had improved significantly.

Our spats at home never lasted long. We both are forgiving. Realizing that we needed all the extra energy we could muster to get through that day's climb, Muir Pass, we made amends and continued our hike.

We began climbing steeply out of the lush, forested meadow and headed above the trees. We were in Evolution Basin.

The sun had shot the mercury into the 80s. During one of our rests, we slathered our exposed skin with sunscreen. By late morning, we were walking along the edge of Evolution Lake. Barren gray mountains stood in every direction, and we saw Mount Darwin, named after Charles Darwin of evolution theory fame. We continued our quest over Muir Pass, staying above 10,000 feet. The trail wound around Sapphire Lake—appropriately named—with its deep, blue, cool water. A distant snow-patched mountain peak across the lake gave a cool sensation despite the warm weather. We stopped for lunch in an open grass-covered area and leaned up against a rock to block the wind.

In spite of the wind, the sun was beginning to take a toll. Although we were covering our skin each day with sunscreen, Beth had developed heat rash on her hands. She now was wearing gloves to decrease sun exposure. The plastic nosepiece of my cheap sunglasses had thinned in the intense sun and finally disintegrated, and the glasses fell from my face to the ground. This really made us realize the damaging effects of the sun. Beth was relying on the rim of her baseball cap to shade her eyes, and she gave me her wire-rimmed sunglasses to wear.

As we marched on, we could see a manmade stone building, Muir Hut, which marked the summit of Muir Pass in the distance. This round building with a cone-shaped roof was assembled entirely from stone and cement by the Sierra Club in memory of John Muir. We could see the hut, but it seemed forever before we finally reached it. Each time the trail leveled off, we thought we had reached the hut, only to discover more trail with the hut still farther off in the distance. By early afternoon, we summitted Muir Pass—at 11,955 feet, our highest pass yet—and took refuge inside the hut for a break. There was a stone fireplace on the wall with a metal dedication plaque mounted above it. A wooden bench lined the circumference of the room.

We slipped out of our packs, sat down on the bench, and broke out a Snickers bar to share.

"Honey, I think I'm getting a blister," Beth complained.

Blisters—especially on your feet—are one of the most painful maladies a hiker can experience. Until this expedition, painful blisters have marred every hike I'd ever taken. Such was the case during the beginning of my Appalachian Trail journey, during which I acquired the trail name Wrong-foot. I know I'm not alone with this dilemma because almost every hiker's backpack contains an array of blister-relieving products. Needless to say, I was pleasantly surprised to realize that we had walked more than half of the John Muir Trail and I had not had one blister, not even so much as a hot spot. Beth and I had been outfitted with Lowa boots courtesy of our boot sponsor, Gore-Tex. I finally had found the best pair of boots for my feet. Wrongfoot no more. Without pain from blisters, I had not even thought about my most important hiking equipment—my feet.

On all of my previous hikes, I primarily worried about my own body and supplies. Even though Beth was in great shape and was carrying her own gear, this was her first long-distance hike, so I paid extra attention to her. I was determined to be the best hiker husband I could so that she would enjoy this trip and want to hike again. Out there, I was not only Beth's husband but her guide as well.

I got off to a bumpy start trying to convince Beth's parents that I was the man who would care for and protect their daughter. Shortly after elevating our friendship to romantic levels, Beth invited me along to meet her family over Thanksgiving. We were only a few months into our romantic relationship, but we knew we were heading toward a long-term commitment. Beth's family figured something was brewing between us because she thought we were serious enough to invite me to meet the entire family—including extended relatives.

Beth, her brothers, their spouses and significant others, and I had gathered at their parents' house for the big meal. We had a few hours before dinner, and I felt the anxiety that one typically feels when meeting his girlfriend's entire family. Needless to say, I felt that I was under the microscope, and like most microorganisms in petri dishes, my imperfections were exposed.

My shortcomings were displayed during what should have been a casual ice-breaking event of tossing the football with Beth's siblings. Paul, Beth's oldest brother, rallied Mike, Brian, Beth, and me out into the front yard for a little play. This was minutes after I met Mike and Paul for the very first time. I'm not much of a football player—I hung up the helmet and shoulder pads in the sixth grade—but what could go wrong with a little game of catch? I positioned myself near the front porch, carefully sidestepping the intricate flowered landscape, while Brian, Paul, Mike, and Beth spread out to the street in a large circle.

The ball passed seamlessly from Paul, to Brian, to Mike, to me, and I tossed it to Beth, who missed it. She had to chase the ball down the street a bit before recovering it and throwing it back to Paul, who passed it to Mike. I stood ready to receive the next pass. Mike tossed the ball, but his aim was ten feet to my right. I was determined to demonstrate my athletic abilities and ran in the direction the ball was sailing. On my route I snapped and squashed an entire bed of flowers that Beth's mom had planted. Beth had inherited her lust for flowers from her mother, who I knew wasn't going to be too pleased when she saw what I had done. Meanwhile, I was still in motion to catch the ball, and I tripped over a rope that had been staked in the ground to support a large pine tree. When I looked back, I saw that the tree lay snapped over on the ground. As I stood assessing the damage I had caused to the yard, I threw the ball to Beth. She was standing in the street and looking toward the house, but she was squinting in the setting sun. Before she could get a good look at the incoming ball, it smacked her in the face. She ran into the house, crying with her hand over her eye. About the only thing I could have done worse at that point was to throw the ball through the front dining room window and bust up Beth's mom's favorite formal china that she had assembled for our meal. Instead, I ran into the house to make sure Beth was all right and apologize to her parents for destroying their yard.

After my grand introduction, if I had suggested to Beth's parents that I would soon marry her and take her on an extreme adventure in the Sierra Nevada, I most likely would have been refused dinner and asked to leave. But Beth and her family eventually knew I was in my element in the mountains. Knowing she would be with me, Beth's parents never once expressed concern for her safety on this adventure.

"Where's the blister?" I asked.

"On my heel. I think it's O.K., though. It doesn't hurt too badly," she replied.

We saddled our packs and began the dramatic descent off

Muir Pass. A little over half a mile from the summit, Beth complained of her blisters again.

"I think the blister is getting worse," she said.

"We need to take a look and see what's going on," I insisted.

We stopped along the trail and took off our packs. Beth perched on the flattest rock she could find and removed her right boot and sock. Her top-layer sock had slipped down off her calf and was all balled up in the front of her boot, which I immediately realized was the reason for the blister. I lifted up her leg to look at her heel, which sported a two-by-two-inch water-filled blister that looked like one of the air-filled pockets in bubble wrap. It would continue to aggravate her if it wasn't popped. I pulled out my first aid kit, took out my Swiss Army knife, and cooked the blade over the heat of my lighter to disinfect the tip, and then I pricked her blister several times to let the water drain out. Popping blisters is a controversial practice. Some hikers recommend letting the blister decrease or pop on its own, but it has been my experience that you can reduce the pain if you pop the blister, as long as you correct the friction that caused it. I applied some antibiotic ointment to the wound, covered it with gauze, and placed a large square of moleskin—a bandage adhesive meant to reduce friction and prevent blisters—over the entire area.

"Have you been pulling your socks up when you retighten your boots?" I asked.

"No," she replied.

"That's why you have this blister," I said. "It's not from the boots."

Beth is a quick learner, and whenever I retightened my boots during one of our breaks, she would do the same. She must not have noticed that I always pulled up my socks before retying my boots. I wanted to make sure we had addressed the problem so it wouldn't happen again. I knew it wasn't the boots because she would have had blisters from Day One. It was the socks bunching up in the front of her boot that forced her heel to rub on the leather.

While we sat performing blister repair, I felt as if I was being watched. I looked over my shoulder and noticed a yellow marmot peeking at us from a rock. He watched as if he was concerned for Beth's foot and wanted to make sure we were all right. Beth pulled her sock up and put her boot back on.

"Are you going to be O.K.?" I asked.

"Yes. Thank you," she said.

We slipped our arms back into our pack straps and stood, hoisting our loads and heading down the trail. I was more agile with my footwork than Beth and was able to descend at a quicker pace, so I was ahead of her on our way down from Muir Pass. We were rapidly descending along a narrow trail that zigzagged along the very edge of the mountain. If you were to watch us from afar, we probably looked like marbles zipping back and forth down a ramp in a plastic game set. The trail was a few feet wider than shoulder width, with a steep, rocky slope climbing up from the trail on one side and a dramatic drop-off on the other side. Nothing stood between us and a fatal plunge down several thousand feet but a row of shin-high rocks.

I had a rhythm going as I hiked. My hiking poles created a metallic clicking sound as I spiked them into the rocky ground for stability. Between the wind hissing in my ears and the clicking of my poles, I barely heard Beth scream. I stopped short and turned. Beth was about fifteen yards behind me, completely upside down, feet sticking up in the air with her head stuck between some rocks on the cliff's edge. I ran back toward her. Oh, my God, please don't fall, I thought. I reached her in seconds and grabbed her by her legs to make sure she didn't fall. I helped her slip her arms out of her pack and lifted her head out from between two boulders. Another five inches and Beth would have gone over the edge of the trail and bounced down the mountainside, not hitting bottom for at least a mile.

"Are you O.K.?" I demanded with fear in my voice.

"I think I hurt my leg," Beth said, tears running down her cheeks.

Her pant leg was torn, and blood trickled from her knee. She was lucky that she didn't smack her head on the rocks. Her pack must have cushioned her head like an airbag in a car. Her leg looked cut.

"Can you walk?" I asked.

Beth stumbled on the trail and then demonstrated a few normal steps. We sat there for a few minutes to catch our breath.

"What happened?" I asked.

"I tripped and flipped forward down the trail," Beth replied.

"Are you babying your blistered foot?"

"Kind of."

We were up near 11,000 feet, with several miles of cliff-edge switchbacks yet to go. There was no way I could carry Beth's gear; there was no place to set up camp, and we were fully exposed to all the elements on this narrow trail. Beth was pretty shaken from her close call, but we had to continue our descent and get below the trees before stopping for the day. I dug out some ibuprofen tablets from my pack and gave them to her.

"Here, take these," I insisted.

Beth swallowed the pills and chased them with a slug of water.

"You can't baby your blistered foot up here, not with a pack on your back. You will fall again if you don't balance your load on both feet," I lectured.

"But my foot hurts," she cried. Tears trickled from her eyes, but they dried instantly on her cheeks in the intense sun.

"There's no way we'll make it down this mountain safely unless you balance your gait and stop leaning on your good foot. Your pack is too heavy for you to wobble along on one foot. Take the pain," I barked.

If looks could kill, I'd have been dead on the spot. I know I sounded insensitive, but I was concerned only for her safety. She needed to shake off the fall, regain her confidence, and balance her walk.

"Right now, I'm talking to you as your guide and not your husband. Don't baby your foot. TAKE THE PAIN," I demanded with as much drill sergeant in my voice as I could muster. I let Beth lead, and I followed. Our four-boot team continued, a little slowly at first.

Beth's blisters healed within a couple of days, and after her fall she always pulled up her socks when she retied her boots. It was her only blister experience during the entire journey. As I reflect back on the moment, I realize how quickly things can go wrong in our lives and that no matter how shaken we are, it is important to get back on our feet. Both feet. When we try to lean unnaturally to avoid a painful situation, we can exacerbate things. Pain is part of life. It hurts, but it can also make us stronger.

Chapter 17
What Thin Air Can Do

Grouse Meadow, 138 miles from Happy Isles,
August 9, 2003

The farther we descended down Muir Pass, the more confident Beth began to feel. The increase in her stride was noticeable, and soon we had resumed normal speed. We came up behind a retired couple, Rick and Lisa from Windsor, Canada, whom we had met back at Vermilion Valley Resort. They had left Vermilion Valley a day before we had, but they had stopped off at Muir Trail Ranch, a small trail outpost that holds hiker re-supply packages and allows hikers to rejuvenate their spirits.

Rick and Lisa were using homemade broomstick hiking poles. As we shared trail talk, a shiny metallic object in the dirt near Rick's foot caught my eye. Stuck to the end of one of his hiking poles was a large lug nut, the size used to hold on semi truck tires.

"What's the nut on the pole for?" I asked, expecting some sort of scientific explanation.

"The tip broke off of my pole, and one of the ranch hands fixed it by embedding this nut so my pole wouldn't get all busted up from hitting the trail."

It looked ridiculous and must have added several ounces of weight to his pole. That might seem like nothing, but it surely would become apparent after picking the pole up and sticking it in the ground a few thousand times.

"Hikers on the Appalachian Trail use trail names that they get from an experience or personal trait. I'm going to call you 'Lugnut' in my journals, if you don't mind," I said.

Lisa chimed in: "What about me?" She held up her pole so that I could see the big wadded ball of duct tape she had wrapped around the bottom tip of her pole.

"Your trail name is Duct Tape," I responded.

We all laughed—even Beth. She needed a laugh.

Beth and I had walked 20 miles that day from McClure Meadow to Grouse Meadow. We had covered 40 miles in two days and gone up and over some big mountains. Beth was exhausted. We found a campsite in the trees that over-looked a peaceful meadow of knee-high grass, a small, mean-dering stream, and distant granite mountain. Beth was just glad to get off her feet and didn't even care that the mosqui-toes hung in the air like curtains. Her knee was swollen and bruised from her fall. The sun hadn't set yet, so I wanted to try to catch some fish. We quickly set up the tent. I grabbed my fishing pole and walked out into the meadow to throw my line into the stream. I caught five trout in 30 minutes. I brought them back to camp, cleaned them as best I could with my Swiss Army knife, and cooked them in some garlic butter as an appetizer. What a treat. Beth held a trout by the fins as she devoured and savagely eyed another fish in the pan. She was ravenous. We cooked up a freeze-dried chili mac as the main course. We were both fantasizing about food that was out of reach. I salivated for a large steak, and Beth craved pizza and ice cream.

Other than a photographer camped nearby and a family set up farther down the trail, we had the entire meadow all to ourselves. After cleaning up our dinner pans, we stripped out of our trail clothes and zipped into our tent. As we climbed into our sleeping bags, I caught a real whiff of how we both smelled, something between road kill and dirty socks. I wrote in my journal, "A couple who stinks together, stays together—in separate sleeping bags, of course. Pee-yew!"

In the morning, we began our morning ritual of breaking camp. I filled our pot with water for coffee and fired up the stove. We robotically broke camp, deconstructing our tent, cramming our sleeping bags into little sacks, and stuffing everything into our packs while the water simmered. Then we sat on a fallen log to eat breakfast bars and sip our coffee. We heard footsteps, and a woman came into view. She walked rapidly toward us from the direction we planned to head that morning. She stopped at our campsite, trying to catch her breath.

"Do you have any communication?" she blurted out with a panicky urgency in her voice. She was a middle-aged woman with an athletic build.

"What do you need?" I asked. We kept our satellite phone out of sight of other hikers so we wouldn't infringe on anyone trying to get away from it all.

"We have a very sick hiker who needs medical attention," the woman said.

"I have a satellite phone. We can make a call for you." I

assured her.

I pulled out the phone and beckoned the woman into the open meadow. I would get a clear signal and hand her the phone when it connected. The woman was hiking with a group of six. One of the men in her party began to feel ill after climbing above 10,000 feet. Usually with altitude sickness, you feel better if you descend in elevation. But the group had camped at 8,000 feet for two days, and the man still was feeling ill. A doctor in the group determined that he had pulmonary edema—a serious condition in which the lungs fill with fluid. It can be fatal if left untreated. Someone from the group set out the afternoon before in search of help, but the group hadn't heard from him. I reached a 911 operator, who patched us to the national parks dispatcher. The woman explained her medical emergency. Apparently, the hiker who went for help had reached authorities. The dispatcher explained that a mountain rescue team had departed by helicopter en route to the area. The woman introduced herself as Angela, thanked us profusely, and ran back down the trail to her group.

Beth and I dumped our coffee on the ground and haphazardly finished cramming our gear into our packs. We wanted to help out any way we could. We ran—sort of—with our packs bouncing awkwardly so that they pulled uncomfortably on our shoulders and rubbed our hips. We reached the group a half mile or so down the trail. They were camped in a serene, shaded, flat area just off the trail with a strong stream running through. The sick man sat upright against a tree in the shade. He had sickly, pale skin and a nauseated grimace on his face. The man sitting near him was monitoring the sick guy's vital signs.

"Can I help out with anything?" I asked.

The man sitting with the sick guy introduced himself as a physician.

"You could stand in the clearing up by the trail and help signal the helicopter when it comes," the doc directed.

I unclipped my pack straps and dropped my pack near Beth, who already had taken off her pack and was sitting on a fallen tree several yards away from all the commotion. I walked up to the clearing with Angela. Within minutes, we heard a rapid thudding that I would have thought was a grouse, but then a helicopter came into view over a distant mountain. The helicopter circled above like a bird looking for its prey. Then it hovered in one spot above us, dropping like a spider from a web precisely into the small clearing where we stood waving our arms. The rotor blades seemed to miss clipping nearby trees by inches. It was obvious that this pilot had flown into tight spots before. Dust kicked up as the helicopter touched down. Two park officials emerged from the helicopter, each clutching his hat with one hand and carrying a medical bag in the other. Angela led them from the clearing to the sick man.

During all this, Beth remained seated on the log. I walked over to her and sat down, and we watched the medics tend to the sick man. It dawned on me that the sick guy most likely was going to fly out to a hospital and would not have any use for the fuel in his hiking stove. I had spilled my fuel a few days ago and had been rationing what I had left. Beth and I had been stopping midday for lunch in shaded areas to get out of the most intense heat. We would then walk into the evening. The problem with stopping for a long period in the middle of the day was that we would get groggy. To reenergize, I had been boiling water for coffee during these midday breaks, so I used up more cooking fuel than I had anticipated. I asked Angela if the sick man had some extra cooking fuel we could use. She was delighted to share his fuel with us. She opened his pack and fished around before pulling out a red fuel cylinder. I took the cylinder over to my pack, pulled out my fuel bottle, and funneled his fuel into my bottle.

While I was pouring the fuel in my bottle, the opportunistic survival side of my mind kicked in: We could replenish our depleted food supplies with this guy's food, I thought. When I had planned our meals for this trip, I'd underestimated Beth's appetite. Back home, she eats one third of what I eat, and I'd planned our meals accordingly. Shockingly, Beth's appetite had become even with mine. She matched me spoonful for spoonful at every meal, especially since we resupplied. We already had depleted most of the extra snacks I had packed to supplement our meals, and I was beginning to ration and limit our daily food so we would have enough to get to the end. This was a sensitive situation. I didn't want to appear like a vulture savagely preying on the sick man's supplies, so I didn't ask for anything other than the much-needed fuel. I hoped someone in the group would ask us if we wanted any of the food in the man's pack. On the trail, the art of receiving food without actually asking for it is called Yogi-ing. While I was busy funneling fuel, I was oblivious to a conversation Angela had with Beth. What I found out later was that while I was filling my fuel bottle, Angela was asking my wife if we would like any of the man's food. Beth had politely declined Angela's offer. She told Angela that we had plenty of food. The fact was that we barely had enough, but Beth hadn't developed the art of Yogi-ing. Beth had grown accustomed over the years to giving food to hikers we met along the Appalachian Trail as we traveled along on day hikes. This time she was on the other end of the stick, and it hadn't quite soaked in.

I carried the sick man's pack to the helicopter. He was not really aware of everything taking place and had already boarded with the help of the medics. I handed the pack to the pilot, who took it and secured it in an exterior container fixed onto the leg of the helicopter. The pilot asked me to stand on the trail and stop hikers from getting too close to the spinning rotors. In minutes, the helicopter fired up and climbed straight up like the spider scurrying back up its web string. It hovered momentarily before pivoting its nose and vanishing behind a mountain ridge. The thrumming of its spinning rotors grew faint until we could hear it no more.

"We should have asked them for some of his food," I told Beth as we slipped on our packs.

"Angela asked me if we wanted any of the food, but I told her we had plenty."

"Beth, we're rationing our food. You are eating as much as I am, and I didn't plan on that. We have just enough food without any splurges to get us to the end."

We walked on. As we anchored our hiking poles into the trail and placed each step, our stomachs growled with the realization that there was no re-supply point between here and the trail's end without hiking 20 miles out of our way. We would have to deal with our food rations one meal at a time.

I didn't say what I said to make Beth feel bad, but she was silent. She's always quiet when she's upset. Beth internalizes her frustrations, whereas I bitch openly. I was being critical of my own error of not anticipating her increase in appetite.

But it was too late to soak in the past.

"Beth, we'll ask the next hikers we run into if they have any extra food they're willing to sell," I said, trying to make her feel better. I should have left it at that, but I had to insert my boot into my mouth. "And since you turned down the offer for food, it's up to you to ask them."

Beth is shy with strangers, and the thought of asking complete strangers for a handout in the woods made her really nervous.

This food dilemma was no laughing matter. A group of settlers, popularly known as the Donner party, were traveling by wagon train through the Sierra in the 1800s—a few hundred miles north of our location—when they ran out of food and resorted to cannibalism. I certainly didn't think our shortage would come to that. But I also knew myself well enough to know that I get mean when I'm hungry. I hate being hungry. If someone were ever to interrogate me for secret information, all they would have to do is starve me for a few days. I'd give up everything I knew in exchange for a cheeseburger.

As we walked on, we were thankful that our health was intact. Other than a few cuts, scrapes, sunburns, and a blister, we were in top shape. That poor guy who fell ill brought to life the risks we were taking as we chugged on toward Mount Whitney.

Chapter 18
A Creep at 10,000 Feet

Descent from Mather Pass, 150 miles from Happy Isles
August 9, 2003

Our goal for the day was to get over Mather Pass, more than ten miles of nearly vertical ascent to above 12,000 feet. We would climb an arid switchback trail for ten miles up a steep, sloping mountain pass. We were still walking within Kings Canyon National Park, the second of three national parks through which the John Muir Trail snakes. The sun shone in a brilliant blue sky as we clicked our poles into the rocky dirt path. We kicked up dust as we pushed off with each stride, the extra momentum propelling us upward. Morning on the trail was a quiet, peaceful time. Our minds were full of fresh thoughts before the day's heat cooked up our instincts for staying hydrated and hunkering down in the shade whenever possible.

We were walking under the cover of occasional stands of trees with the knowledge that we soon would rise above the tree line for most of the day. Beth and I spotted four hikers making their way along the trail, and we soon caught up with them—two men, each with his college-age son. They were walking the John Muir Trail and had started a day before us. They were taking a standing break under the shade of trees at a small stream crossing. We stopped and socialized for a bit. We ate an energy bar, slugged down some water, and enjoyed the shade as much as we could.

The fathers-and-sons group seemed in good spirits. They were from Los Angeles. One of the fathers was a homicide detective. *Wow,* I thought, *with a career like that in a city like that, I would definitely need routine long-distance hikes.* After our brief trailside chat, we all continued the march upward out of the dense cover of trees. Beth and I pulled ahead of the four men as they began to string out along the trail, each at his own pace. Beth and I struggled to keep an equal pace. At times, Beth was able to ascend in the thin air faster than I. I needed to take frequent breaks as we climbed. Before our trip, Beth had spent months in a spinning class—an organized biking workout—to which she attributed her ability to handle the thinner air. I was beginning to believe she was right.

Since my fishing license kicked in, I had been strapping my fishing rod to the side of my pack for quick access. On this particular morning, I left my hook on the line. I clipped it into one of the loops on the rod so that I could quickly convert from hiker to fisherman as we encountered water. As we walked along, my hook had snagged a nearby tree branch. As I moved along the trail, my fishing line unreeled with every step until the entire reel had completely unwound. When it reached the end of the spinner cast, I was jerked back like a large fish being pulled out of water. Startled, I turned around to see what had pulled me back. I noticed the fishing line leading from my pack back down the trail.

"Beth, hold up!" I shouted.

I dropped my pack off my back, pulled my fishing rod loose from my pack, and began walking back down the trail and reeling in the line. I followed the fishing line down the trail and around several bends for at least 250 feet, untangling the line as I went. It had wound around trees, bushes, and rocks. The four guys we had met earlier caught up as I was reeling in the last of the line. I knew I looked ridiculous, as if I were trying to catch fish on land. They never asked what I was doing as they paused to watch and sip from their water bottles. By the looks on their faces, I could tell they were drawing their own conclusions. I was embarrassed and didn't offer any explanation. The detective and his group passed us and continued up the mountain. I removed my hook and fastened my fishing rod to my pack so it wouldn't happen again.

The sun beat down as we walked on. Our sweat dried almost as soon as it rose to our skin. I detected a strong mint smell as Beth and I climbed higher and higher up Mather Pass. I suspected mint leaves were growing along the trail, and although I had taken several botany classes in college, I couldn't remember what mint plants looked like. We stopped to sip some water and catch our breath, and I could still smell a minty scent. I figured it must have been coming from the nondescript bushes along the trail. I pulled a leaf from one of the bushes and bit into it. The leaf released a bitter burst of juice, far from the cool mint I had anticipated. I gulped water, spit, and swished my mouth several times with more water. The taste lingered for quite some time. I knew better than to nibble on vegetation unless I was sure of its species, and I was reminded why.

Beth and I could see the detective and the three other

men, now high above us, shifting back and forth along the steep switchback trail. A man in a deep green uniform came into view and was heading toward us down the pass. A gold emblem on his chest identified him as a park ranger. As we rounded the bend of a switchback, we stopped to let the park ranger pass us. He stopped and introduced himself. He was returning from his routine foot patrol. He was based out of Le Conte Canyon, a small outpost below us along the middle fork of Kings River. This was the ranger whom the sick hiker's party had tried to locate earlier. They were unsuccessful because he had left for an overnight patrol.

The ranger said he was filming a documentary about John Muir Trail hikers. He asked us if he could interview us about why we were hiking the John Muir Trail. He mentioned that he had met a hiker on the other side of Mather Pass who was uneasy about being filmed and whose manner was rude and abrupt. The ranger seemed nervous that we might refuse an interview as well. We assured him that we were more than happy to share the mission behind our journey. This was a good opportunity to talk about Mike and to discuss depression symptoms and treatment, including exercise and sun exposure. Beth did most of the talking—which was unusual—and gave a great interview.

As we continued our climb, we noticed fresh droplets of blood the size of pennies splashed sporadically on the rock slab steps that had been assembled on the trail. Nosebleeds are common in the dry, thin air, and that most likely was the source of the blood. But I kept wondering what was going through the homicide detective's mind as he followed the trail of blood up the pass.

The trail leveled off and skirted the Palisade Lakes. We stopped for a break to refill our water bottles and eat lunch. I decided to fish. I removed my rod from my pack, reattached a hook and fly, and flung my rod behind my head. I snapped it forward and hit the release button to cast. All of my casting motions were perfect, but the fly and hook didn't extend as expected. Instead, the entire spinner casing—the plastic base-ball-size contraption that contained the fishing line—somehow released from the pole and shot out into the water. At the beginning of our expedition, I had to buy a new spinner because the original one had been damaged in our baggage on the trip out. Apparently, I didn't attach the spinner to the pole properly. So instead of lofting a hook and fly lightly into the water to trick a trout, I made a tremendous splash that sent shockwaves across the pond.

"I'm tricking the fish with the ol' bomb-shell effect," I quipped as I felt Beth look up from the book she was reading while perched on a nearby rock. She rolled her eyes and grinned, not buying one word. I reattached the spinner and untangled the line, and I still managed to pull in two trout. It could only have been the work of God helping me recover some respect as a polished outdoorsman.

Before moving along, we took a Snickers break and called our webmaster on the satellite phone to give her an update on our progress and adventures. I left out my stupid fishing mishaps. Georgia said that our website had logged thousands of hits and that some of our family members had been calling and e-mailing her for updates. They weren't satisfied with the speed at which we were reporting our progress to Georgia. With the compassion of a preacher's wife, Georgia responded to our families' anxious requests for information. We knew we had a great person handling our communications while we were on the trail.

We still had miles to go to the summit of Mather Pass,

which we could see in the distance. It was a grayish, barren, steep and rocky mountain with patches of white snow persisting in the intense sun. It was hard to believe there were trails winding up these mountains. From a distance, they looked impassable, like vertical rock piles. The trail crews had cleared zigzagging paths. They moved aside thousands of rocks and stacked them to reinforce the cliff-edge footing. With each mile, I grew more respectful of the laborious efforts of the trail crews to construct this path.

We reached the summit of Mather Pass, 12,100 feet, by late afternoon. It was named in honor of Stephen Mather, the first man to head the National Park Service. We could see for miles to distant mountains and beyond. Lakes and ponds looked like scant water droplets, and trees were like blades of grass. We spent several minutes taking in the view we had spent the day approaching before we descended the steep switchback trail on the other side. Although the views were awesome, the last thing we wanted was to be up on a pass at nightfall. The weather was so unpredictable, and there was barely space for safe walking, let alone a suitable spot to pitch a tent. The simple act of relieving yourself in the night could prove fatal with one misstep.

As we descended, the sun drew closer and glared across the mountain. After a few miles of steep switchbacks, the trail leveled out into an area known as Upper Basin. It was speckled with ponds, streams, and grass but no trees. We stopped next to a truck-size boulder on the shoulder of the trail for a rest. We had hiked more than 12 hard miles in the blazing sun since our drama-filled morning with the sick hiker. We sat and leaned up against the large rock, relieving the pack weight from our backs without removing them. As we snacked on candy bars and eyed the map for possible campsites, we caught sight of a silhouette. We were facing the setting sun, and its glare prevented us from focusing, but we could make out a person walking toward us across a pathless, barren, flat landscape. He was at least a quarter of a mile away and must have spotted us coming down the pass. Why would a person walk a quarter of a mile to confront complete strangers? Maybe something was wrong. The person was definitely headed in our direction. The sun let off a steaming glare behind him, and we squinted anxiously. What did he want?

I knew that we were safer out in the mountains—safer from being victimized by humans, anyway—than if we were living in Mayberry. But I remembered something a federal agent told me several years before when I reported a creepy hiker on the Appalachian Trail. He had said, "Charles Manson was arrested by park rangers in a California national park." I didn't want to worry Beth, but I wasn't taking any chances. The man was 200 yards out and closing in. I realized that in my sitting position, weighted down with a heavy pack on my back, I was vulnerable and incapable of defending us if need be. I stood up and unscrewed the circular basket from the tip of my hiking pole, turning it into a makeshift spear. I unzipped my hip pouch and armed Beth with my pepper spray, instructing her to have it ready. I unclipped my pack straps in case I needed to slip out of the pack quickly, and I stood tall and puffed out my chest, like a soldier at attention. I tried to look as intimidating and confident as possible and to hide my completely exhausted state.

The sun's glare deflected as the man got within a few feet of us. He was wearing a red-and-white checkered flannel shirt and blue jeans—cotton is a big no-no for mountain survival. He had dark skin, long brown hair, and a stout, muscular build. He got within ten feet of us and stopped. He stood facing us but never made direct eye contact.

"Hi," I said.

"Hey, there," he crackled back in an eerily low pitch.

Beth stayed seated in silence, holding the pepper spray discreetly in one hand with her trigger finger ready.

"Did you guys run into that ranger with the video camera?" he asked.

"Yeah, he's filming a documentary," I replied.

"I told him to get away from me and that I didn't want anything to do with his camera," the man retorted angrily.

So this was the guy the ranger had told us about. I felt sick. Why was he so concerned about avoiding contact with a ranger but had enough ambition to walk across a barren meadow to confront us? Something wasn't adding up.

"Where are you from?" I asked.

"Not from around here," the man responded. He sounded cocky, and he stepped closer.

I held my hiking pole with both hands like a soldier grasping a bayonet-tipped rifle. In my mind, I played out my actions should this guy try anything. I would spear him in the chest with my pole with all my might, drop my pack, grab Beth and lurch upwind from the man. We would douse him with pepper spray and hog-tie him with duct tape. Then we would run as fast as we could down the trail until we were out of sight, sneak off behind some rocks, call 911 on the satellite phone, and send our GPS coordinates. It seemed like it could work.

"So where do you live?" I demanded.

"Canada," he said.

That's a hell of an address, I thought. *Canada is a big country.*

"What are you doing out here?"

"Camping out for a while," he said.

"We're with a big group walking the John Muir Trail as an awareness campaign for depression," I half-lied. "We're posting our progress on a website as we go along and are in communication with a ground control crew." I wanted him to think that there were others with us on the trail in case he had any bad intentions and that we'd be missed immediately if anything happened to us.

"Why don't you two come back to my camp for the night?" he asked.

Yeah, right. That was the last thing we'd do. We couldn't see any sign of a camp anywhere. For all we knew, he could have a bloody axe stashed across the field and had been waiting to lure victims into his trap. This was the sort of guy that you would want your children to run screaming from if he pulled up in a car and offered a ride. We wanted to get as far away from him as possible.

"No, thanks. We still have several miles to go before we stop," I answered.

"All right, see ya later then." He turned into the sun and again became a silhouette as he retreated along the barren landscape.

"Come on, Beth. Let's get out of here."

We walked rapidly down the trail and hoped we would never see that man again. I felt uneasy and wondered if he would follow us. I kept looking back over my shoulder.

A few miles later, we ran into two young guys, Doug and Rick, who had been out for a day and were returning to their base camp. They were camped a few miles down the trail, so we walked along with them. These guys seemed safe. They were new graduates from the East who had taken jobs in L.A. and were just starting to make their marks on the world. I asked them if they would mind if we pitched camp near their base camp. There was strength in numbers, and I told them about the creep we encountered. They were fine with that.

We dropped under the canopy of trees and soon reached a serene campsite along a whitewater stream. We felt relieved to be camping near these guys. Doug noticed my Appalachian Trail patch, and that sparked a conversation that lasted well into the evening. He was from Boston and had done some hiking on the AT. The two worked in the film industry, splicing and assembling movies. It sounded like a neat career. Night fell rapidly, and we drifted off to sleep feeling secure with other campers nearby. The loud white noise of the mountain stream surely would have drowned out our cries for help should the creep tear into our tent in the wee hours. Still, our exhaustion overcame our fear, and we both fell asleep. Early the next morning as we made coffee, Doug and Rick announced they were hiking out of the backcountry to return to civilization. This was our cheesy opportunity to ask them if they had any leftover meals they could sell us to supplement our short food supply. We were in luck. They sold us two freeze-dried entrees of two servings each. We wished them luck in their careers and thanked them profusely for the food.

God works in magical ways. Even out in the remote wilderness, we were experiencing trail magic when we really needed it. When we feared harm from the creep, we ran into other hikers and felt safe, and we didn't have to worry about running out of food.

Chapter 19
Nomadic Healing

Arrowhead Lake, 169 miles from Happy Isles
August 10, 2003

In 1998, I walked the 2,160-mile Appalachian Trail solo, with no one to share in conversation for most of the journey, no one to share the burden of carrying the heavy camp items, no one to hold close when sounds in the dark woods pierced the nylon tent walls. Although walking all that way by oneself might sound lonely and frightening, it actually was an unbelievable experience. I talked to everyone I encountered to satisfy my socialization shortfall. I adjusted to carrying all the camp gear. And I soon learned to recognize practically every sound that went bump in the night. My thoughts bounced all over the place as I drifted along. I had some revolutionary thoughts. I contemplated business strategies and tried to solve the world's crises, but most of all I was able to enjoy being removed from outside influences and was able to tunnel into my inner core and find out who I was. Most folks live their entire lives without ever taking time out to discover their individuality. My thoughts also covered the basics: what I was going to eat for dinner, how many Snickers bars did I have left until the next town, where I was going to stop for the night.

Beth and I joined in marriage a year after my AT thru-hike. Although it would have been more reassuring to me if Beth had some backpacking excursions on her life experience resume, she did have quite an athletic past as an accomplished marathoner. I figured she would eventually throw on a backpack and give long-distance hiking a shot. Besides, she was the only girl among three older brothers, and that made her a bit of a tomboy.

Beth and I were (and still are) happily married, but we hadn't yet bonded nomadically. That might sound ridiculous to most people, but I spent half a year living in the woods and styling my life around the hiking culture, so to me, this was an important aspect of our relationship. In addition to walking for an important cause, Beth was finally indoctrinating herself into the thru-hiking community. She and I also were experiencing our relationship from a whole new angle—having to rely on each other for daily survival. We were a team; we had to be in order to complete this expedition. We supported and encouraged each other. We kept in step with each other; we split the burden of pack weight. At the same time, I was anxious about how we would get along on such an expedition. My last long-distance excursion was solo, and I knew I could make this trek alone, but I really wanted the experience of hiking with Beth. I wanted it to be such a positive experience that we both would want to come back and backpack overnight together regularly. But I didn't really know how Beth would enjoy our adventure. She was in great physical shape, but how would she adapt to the daily pain, dirt, sweat, and hunger, without a television, phone, or hot shower for weeks on end?

We were well into our third week, and Beth was handling the trail hardships well. Sometimes too well. She was emerging from the urban ways she had known all her life. She was completely out of her comfort zone and was realizing she could do this. Perhaps this was just the outside-of-the-box challenge she needed. Hiking with a companion is still at times very much an individual experience with nature.

A day earlier, we had climbed to our highest elevation yet, Mather Pass, and today we would climb even higher over Pinchot Pass at 12,130 feet. The oxygen was decreasing with each mountain pass as we slowly progressed higher and higher toward Mount Whitney. Summiting Pinchot Pass would put 157 miles behind us on some of the most rugged high-elevation terrain in the United States. We had just 60 miles to go. Although the end was in sight on the map, several mountainous obstacles stood in the way. The highest elevation of our adventure was yet to come.

We left the cool comforts of our shaded campsite. We had camped just five miles from the summit of Pinchot Pass, but the rest of the way was almost straight up. Our pace slowed noticeably as we climbed, and we were taking more breaks. We would walk for several hundred yards and then stop briefly to stabilize our breathing before pushing ahead. It felt like we needed to take two breaths to capture the same amount of oxygen as one breath back home at sea level. My testosterone was in check because I seemed to be the one initiating all the stops on the uphills.

The sky was blue with only sparse cloud cover. We hadn't

had rain since the first few days of our expedition. The trees grew sparse the higher we climbed up the mountain. A marmot lay flat on a large boulder sunning itself and watching us curiously as we passed. As we climbed, we could see a distant mountain of unusual color. The mountain sat stoutly beside another mountain of similar elevation. The first was a dark, brown-sugar color, and in the valley between the two humps, the rock color changed immediately and dramatically. The other mountain was light tan, and together they resembled scoops of chocolate and vanilla ice cream.

We reached the Pinchot Pass summit and were spoiled once again with a bird's-eye view, the reward for a day in the Sierras. We could see across the southern basin we soon would walk. It was sprinkled with trees, ponds, and lakes that were tiny dots and teardrops from above. As we stood snapping photos, we heard the clicking of trekking poles grinding into the trail combined with gravel crunching beneath boots. A gray-haired man and a young woman emerged onto the small, flat summit where we sat. We introduced ourselves and chatted for a while, taking turns snapping pictures of each other. The woman was in her late twenties and said she was a schoolteacher. She was walking with her father, a self-employed electrician. Very cool, I thought, to take your daughter on a rugged journey and to bond in the wild. They were walking a large stretch of the JMT.

I became engrossed in conversation with the father. We discussed important life issues such as what trails we both had hiked, what our favorite trail snacks were, what we were going to eat for dinner that night, how to retire with enough youth left to walk the entire Pacific Crest Trail, etc. I was so focused in conversation that I didn't notice at first what

Beth was doing. Before we left on our expedition, a friend of Beth's warned her that the thin mountain air would increase the occurrence of a woman's menstrual cycle. In response to the advice, Beth stockpiled large quantities of feminine products—enough to outfit a squad of cheerleaders—that filled an entire compartment of her backpack. She had picked up even more at our halfway re-supply. Realizing now that she was a little too gung ho, Beth was now educating the guy's daughter about the thin-air effect. The father-daughter team had been in the woods only a few days. So the next thing you know, Beth was unloading a large portion of her feminine product inventory from her pack and into the young woman's pack. On the streets of L.A. or New York, Beth might have looked rather suspicious passing zip-locked, gallon-size baggies stuffed full of white tubes discreetly from her pack to another, but for Beth, this was business: she was lightening her load and freeing up pack space.

The woman asked Beth about our "Hike For Mike" shirts, and Beth started a conversation about our awareness expedition. She explained how thousands were following our expedition from our website as we posted daily journals via satellite phone. She also explained that walking the John Muir Trail was a great way to help get the word out because walking and exposure to the sun can help decrease depression symptoms. The woman's dad perked up at Beth's explanation.

"We think my son has depression," he said. "We would like to get him out here hiking with us. It would do him some good."

We suggested that the man encourage his son to see a doctor and gave them our web address before saying our goodbyes and heading in opposite directions. We began to descend

Pinchot Pass. We continued south and dropped dramatically in elevation, down to around 8,500 feet. We rock-hopped across a few streams and walked for several more miles. We came upon a livestock drift fence blocking the trail. Wire twine and barbed wire were wrapped around shoulder-high logs, and we had to stop and carefully untangle the wire to open the gate wide enough for us to squeeze through. We refastened the gate when we were through. The fence line meandered across a sparsely covered green pasture. We had encountered these fences every so often since the beginning of the trail which are used to keep the horses and mules from drifting.

Farther along the trail, we heard the distant clap of water crashing onto rocks as we approached Woods Creek. A dramatic bridge came into view. It stretched high above the water and saved us from having to ford the treacherous stream. The bridge was suspended by cables with a shoulder-width foot walk. A sign read: One Person at a Time on Bridge. This was known as the Golden Gate of the Sierra. In spite of its rugged, one-person limit and rudimentary wood and cable architecture, it did indeed resemble San Francisco's Golden Gate. The irony for us was that the Golden Gate Bridge is one of the world's most notorious places to commit suicide. The Golden Gate has gained such notoriety for suicide jumpers that entire organizations have been created to help prevent jumpers from taking the plunge. In an effort to stop the jumpers, phones have been installed along the bridge so people can call for help, and police officers patrol regularly. The farther we walked along the John Muir Trail, the more we began to suspect that it was our destiny to take this journey to call attention to the devastating and sometimes deadly effects of untreated depression.

We crossed the Golden Gate of the Sierra, which was like a rite of passage along our depression awareness journey. To the fisherman nearby, the bridge was nothing more than an access from one side of the whitewater stream to the other. For us, though, it was as if God knew we would one day take the JMT pilgrimage to get the word out about depression. The tough part about depression is that many times the symptoms aren't recognized by the person experiencing them or by those around him, and that even if the person knows he is depressed, he keeps it to himself. It's a foolish thing, considering the fact that most depression cases can be treated with the same confidential drill of seeing a doctor as for any other illness.

Beth and I trekked into the evening. We approached a pond-sized body of water called Dollar Lake. A rounded-tipped mountain called Painted Lady reflected its image across the mirror-like water. We continued walking as the sun descended until we found a majestic campsite along the shore of Arrowhead Lake, another pond-like lake lined with pine trees and a mountain wall on the opposite shore. It was a perfect place to stop for the night.

We set up camp, inflated our Therm-a-Rests, pulled our sleeping bags out of their stuff sacks, and selected a freeze-dried dinner entrée. Beth complained that she could smell her own stink. "I feel disgusting!" she exclaimed loud enough for some hikers camped well over a hundred yards away to look over.

Before our trip, I had imagined an intimate three-week adventure full of frequent skinny-dipping excursions in the lakes along the way. In reality, though, the lakes were extremely cold, cold enough to anatomically alter even the most well endowed male. At the end of each day, instead of jumping into these cold lakes, we had gotten into the habit of wiping the grime, sand, dust, dried sweat, and bug repellent off our bodies with travel towelettes, and we took controlled sponge baths in which we strategically splashed minimal amounts of the glacial water onto our bodies. Ever since our hike began, we had been averaging 20-mile days and were extremely tired and hungry at night. We wanted nothing more than to clean off the grime, eat dinner, write in our journals, climb in our sleeping bags, and fall asleep. We barely had the energy to give each other a good night kiss.

After our camp was set up, Beth shocked me. "I can't take this grimy feeling," she pronounced. She marched over to the lakeshore, kicked off her boots, and jumped in, clothes and all, with a big splash. Our neighbors nearby watched in amazement, knowing full well how cold the water was. Beth dunked her head under and waded around. Refusing to be showed up by my wife, I kicked off my boots, walked over and waded into the water. It was cold enough to chill beer. Beth stood in the water looking over at me smiling with an exhilarated look. After a few moments, we both climbed out, dripping wet with the cool evening air chilling us even more. We removed our wet clothes, hung them on a line I tied between two nearby bushes, and put on dry sets of long underwear. We boiled water and prepared a freeze-dried meal. Then we zipped into our tent to keep each other warm.

Chapter 20
Walking as One

Ascent of Forester Pass, 184 miles from Happy Isles
August 11, 2003

One of the main differences between the Appalachian Trail and the John Muir Trail that I noticed was the number of people on the JMT as compared to the AT. Sure, we were encountering hikers almost every day, but the Appalachian Trail sees millions of people setting foot each year, and not just in overrun tourist areas. I saw people every day of my AT hike. Hundreds of roads intersect the 2,160-mile Appalachian Trail, so it's easy to walk a swath of AT wilderness. That was one of the reasons for the creation of the AT: to make the wilderness easily accessible to urbanites. Conversely, the John Muir Trail doesn't cross a single road for its entire 218 miles. The JMT is considerably shorter than the AT, but even the AT's most remote section, a 100-mile wilderness in Maine, is intersected by logging roads at several points. Come to think of it, Beth and I hadn't run into cotton-clad, flip-flop-wearing tourists since leaving Yosemite

National Park weeks ago. Even when we share camp, the other campers space themselves so far away it's as if they're not even there. Not that I have anything against roads and people. I often use those very roads along the AT to revisit my favorite sections, and I enjoy most of my social encounters with others while in the great outdoors.

The sun illuminated our tent walls bright and early. I unzipped the rain fly over our tent, and Beth rolled over, signaling the start of a new day. In the four years we have been married, I have never seen Beth fall back asleep in the morning. I, on the other hand, have no problem realizing I'm still tired and plunking my head down for a few more hours of zzz's. My ancestors must have invented the snooze button—probably to annoy Beth's ancestors who didn't sleep in. We peeked our heads out of the tent, still lying on our bellies with our upper bodies propped up on our elbows. The view across the lake was awesome. The morning sun reflected the brilliant blue sky and mountains off the glassy lake. Neither of us wanted to unzip from our warm bags and step out into the crisp morning air. But this was a perfect coffee moment, so we finally broke free from our warm bags to make breakfast.

Our camp at Arrowhead Lake was on the ascent to Glen Pass, an 11,978-foot mountain crest, with less than four miles to the top. We slowly packed up and began walking upward around 8 a.m. Each morning, we would start out wearing jackets, long pants, and hats. But we ended up peeling off the layers down to shorts and T-shirts after a mile or so. We walked along a series of lakes known for their good fishing. We recognized a hiker resting on a rock 20 yards from the trail. He had been at Vermilion Valley Resort—our half way re-supply point—when we were there. We waved as we passed, and he waved back. After leaving the lakes, the trail climbed quickly above tree line on a series of switchbacks. We would walk a few hundred yards, pause, catch our breath, and continue. The upper portions of Glenn Pass looked man-made, like a pile of broken, jagged rocks that had been neatly stacked into a mountain—perhaps God's version of Legos or Lincoln Logs. From a distant view, it was hard to fathom that a trail actually wound its way up through such rubble. But in fact, a graded trail zigzagged all the way to the top. We could see hikers on the crest looking down at us as we climbed, and we were still a mile from the top.

We summitted Glen Pass by late morning. The wind gusts whistled in our ears and whipped our hair around with enough strength to throw us off balance if we weren't careful. Beth and I sat down to stabilize ourselves and pulled out a snack. We had been leapfrogging hikers all along the climb. When we stopped, someone would pass us, and a short time later, we would pass that person stopped for a rest. We sat near two young men, one of whom was the guy we saw on the rock earlier. They were research scientists from Berkeley taking a summer break from the lab. We sat and chatted for a while. They noticed our "Hike For Mike" shirts and asked who Mike was. Beth explained. They wrote down our web address to check out when they got home. We corresponded with them several times after our hike.

A young woman climbed up onto the ridge and was excited to see another female on the trail. She walked up to Beth and introduced herself. I thought for sure Beth was going to pitch the thin-air effect in hopes of eliminating more feminine products, but this time, Beth was on the hunt for toilet paper. Let me say that nothing is more of a commodity in the woods than toilet paper. There is nothing more uncomfortable than having to resort to cold, wet leaves. I witnessed an AT thru-hiker quit his long-distance pilgrimage shortly after running out of toilet paper and having to resort to snow-covered leaves. Beth's TP supply had dwindled down near the end of her roll, and we still had a few days left of our expedition. Before leaving camp that morning, Beth had asked me how much TP I had as we packed up. I showed her my slim roll and explained that I had just enough to finish the trail.

"Do you have any extra toilet paper you could spare?" Beth asked the young woman hiker after we had chatted for a while. Beth has never been one to ask for handouts, and I could tell by the uncertainty in her voice that she was nervous about asking someone for TP but desperate enough to step out of her comfort zone. I think Beth would've rather run out of food than TP.

"We will let you call anyone anywhere from this ridge with our satellite phone in trade," she added, trying to seal the deal.

That was too good an offer to pass up. The woman's face lit up as she pulled out a roll of TP, handed it to Beth, and said, "Take as much as you like. I've got plenty more."

I pulled out our satellite phone, dialed in the number of her choice, and she talked away. As we descended Glen Pass, I couldn't help but replay Beth's mountaintop business deal. "Two mountaintops, two successful business deals. I'm afraid to contemplate what you will barter for on the last two mountains," I joked. Beth kept walking, basking in her success.

On the decent, the sun became intense, so we found a small stand of trees and took cover for a rest. We decided to take a long siesta in the shade to beat the heat. We pulled our Therm-a-Rest pads out of our packs, inflated them, and lay down for an hour. I felt lazy just lying there at midday, but the thought of walking in the heat squelched my anxieties. After lying down, it was hard to get motivated to walk again. So I fired up the stove, boiled some water, and prepared a beef stew, one of the meals we purchased from the film producers a few days ago. I made some coffee with the remaining water. With this burst of fuel firing through our bodies, we slung on our packs and continued our descent.

Around midafternoon, we had descended below tree line, out of the sun and across occasional cool streams. We rounded a bend in the trail near Bubbs Creek and encountered five sweaty men dressed in khaki shirts and wide-brimmed, blue plastic construction hats with the initials "CCC" plastered all around the rims. Could this actually be the real deal, a Civilian Conservation Corps hard at work under the payroll of the federal government? In 1933 during the Great Depression, President Franklin Delano Roosevelt created the Civilian Conservation Corps, nicknamed Roosevelt's Tree Army, to help the severely depressed economy by employing thousands of jobless young men to plant trees to stop erosion caused by decades of careless clear-cutting of forest. The CCC built roads, trails, fortified national parks and forestlands with shelters and buildings, helped out in natural disasters, and much more. Every state employed the CCC, whose ranks topped 600,000 in its heyday. Chances are good that you have walked on a trail, driven on a road, or been in a building constructed by the CCC. The corps was a positive energy for America during the height of the Depression, and it championed a great cause: helping to preserve nature and our awesome national park system. As a matter of fact, I believe that our welfare system should be modeled after the CCC to give a sense of dignity and pride to those in need of work or government assistance. But I thought the CCC had been abolished at the onset of World War II. Could Beth and I have stepped into a time warp? Would we find Model Ts rambling down the road when we came out of the woods?

As we approached, I looked for signs of modern equipment that would squelch my sci-fi thoughts. The men were hard at work swinging hammers and picks, lifting shovels full of rocks, and dropping them into a log-reinforced section of trail they were building. Someone shouted, "Let the hikers pass," as we approached, and the work paused.

"Hey, guys, are you with the Civilian Conservation Corps?" I asked, as Beth and I stepped through their work area.

One of the men responded, "No, we work for the California Conservation Corps." In 1976, California created its own conservation corps modeled after Roosevelt's Tree Army. I asked the crew for permission to take their picture and thanked them for their hard work, and we continued on.

The trail proceeded beneath forest canopy along Bubbs Creek, a great area to pitch camp with plenty of shade and water. We had walked almost a mile since encountering the CCC, and we sat down for a rest. I pulled out our maps and realized that we had just completed Map 3 and were now on Map 2. "Beth, we are on our last two maps!" I exclaimed. We started our trip on Map 13 in Yosemite National Park and had followed a red line across each 8-by-11-inch waterproof plastic topography map. These maps had been great for marking our progress by completing one sheet and moving to the next. We were re-energized with the reality that we were near the end of our expedition. Map 2 was entirely devoted to the ascent and descent of Forester Pass, and Map 1 was the topography for Mount Whitney. Only two more mountain passes left, although they were the two highest passes along the entire JMT. With at least five hours of daylight left, we had to make a decision. Do we keep moving along or stop for the day? We agreed to keep on trekking. Beth had not yet shied away from a long, hard day of hiking. We took a break to look at the map and decided what we wanted to do. From here we would leave the shade once again and climb above tree line.

We continued along our ascent of Forester Pass. This would be the first time we had attempted to summit two passes in one day. Before that day, each day was marked by a full day's climb up and over a pass then camping in valleys and canyons to set us up to tackle the next pass the following day. I just hoped we weren't biting off more than we could chew. Forester Pass is the highest pass along the Pacific Crest Trail at over 13,000 feet. After clearing tree line, there would be little opportunity for camping among miles of boulder fields and narrow switchback trail.

We stopped at a creek-side campsite to replenish our water and make a last decision as to whether we were able to continue. We had at least four miles of steep, sun-exposed ascent to the top, and then another four or five miles of dramatic decent on the other side. It was late afternoon. We had our work cut out for us. A middle-aged couple sat resting on a car-size boulder in the campsite where we stopped. We introduced ourselves. I left Beth with them and went down to the creek to pump water. The couple, Kiley and Rick, were from California and had walked the JMT together several times. They were taking a rest before tackling Forester Pass. Knowing they were planning to tackle Forester Pass reassured us that we weren't out of our minds to attempt such a hike so late in the day. Of course, they could be off their rockers.

While I was pumping water from the stream, Peter Baldwin, the defender of the JMT speed record, zipped by. I was down in the trees to pump water and missed him. Beth, Kiley, and Rick said he was wearing a small hip pack typically used by day hikers, with a Therm-a-Rest sleeping pad attached, trail running shoes, and a ball cap with a sunscreen flap on the back. This guy had set out to break his very own JMT speed record of just a little over four days. Beth and I had set three weeks aside to complete the trail, and three weeks is considered fast for the hike. Baldwin had waited until a full moon to begin his trek so that he could see better at night. We later learned that he did indeed break his old record with a new standing of 94 hours and 4 minutes, or 3.91 days. He slept only two hours a day, running most of the trail with a support team meeting him occasionally to re-supply his morale and food. I prefer my slower method of backcountry travel, but I admire his passion and drive. A rule from the woods that I try to implement in my everyday life is that everyone should hike his own hike.

Beth and I followed Kiley and Rick up Forester Pass. It was refreshing to walk with another couple who had been backpacking together for a while.

"Kiley leads because her pace is slower than mine," Rick said. Beth and I silently took note, having encountered some frustration with keeping pace with each other.

"Do you have children?" I asked.

"We have a daughter in high school," Kiley responded.

"Does she ever hike with you?"

"When she was younger, we took her camping, but she never took interest in backpacking," Kiley responded.

With the incredible pace they were walking, it was no wonder their daughter declined to hike with them. She probably couldn't keep up. Beth and I could barely stay close enough to carry a conversation within earshot. Kiley and Rick, with their experience walking the JMT several times together, were walking perfectly in step, like a four-legged animal. They planned to cross over Forester, descend down to the first table of flat land, and pitch camp. Beth and I didn't have a bivouac plan—we were just focused on getting over the pass. The distance between us and Kiley and Rick grew as they pulled further ahead. They became bug-sized dots zigzagging up the steep, narrow pass. Pebbles kicked up from their boots would click like marbles off the mountainside, reminding us how high and steep this pass was. Each switchback was one gradually inclining shelf above another.

Beth and I slowly huffed up to the summit in time to burn one of the prettiest sunsets into our memories. We must have just missed Kiley and Rick because we could hear their voices echoing up from their canyon descent on the other side. The sky turned the brilliant colors that children select from crayon boxes—deep blues, cottony yellows, burning reds, hunter oranges, and eventually black as the sun fell behind a distant mountain.

Beth was lost in thought as we enjoyed this remarkable sunset. While vacationing with her parents in Seattle, she and Mike had taken advantage of their location and planned a day hike up Mount Sai. They carried water bottles in their hands as they chugged their way to the top. Beth had run cross country in high school and thought she was in such good shape that she could easily run up the mountain and leave Mike in the dust. It was a lot harder than she thought, though. She ran up a couple of switchbacks and quickly became winded. She thought she was going to pass out, so she sat down and waited for Mike. He soon caught up, and they stuck together all the way to the top. They sat and enjoyed the view and their accomplishment. Hunger soon overcame them, and they descended the mountain and found a Dairy Queen. Beth hadn't realized that it was the last mountain she would climb with Mike. But she said later that as she watched the sunset on Forester Pass, she knew he was with her in spirit.

I had to relieve my bladder, but I had few options as Beth and I stood on a narrow piece of ground flanked with dramatic drop-offs on either side. I remembered the pebbles that dropped near us from Kiley's and Rick's boots when they were above us on the trail and ruled out relieving myself on the side of the pass they were traveling down. I would hate to douse one of them and ruin any pleasant memories they had of us. Instead, I turned to the north side, taking the calculated risk of sprinkling a stranger who might just assume the moisture was rain.

Forester Pass was marked with a thick metal sign with white lettering that read: Entering Sequoia National Park, Forester Pass, 13,200 feet. We were leaving Kings Canyon National Park and entering the third and final park of our adventure. Forester Pass is well known among Pacific Crest Trail thru-hikers as the highest pass along their Mexico-to-Canada odysseys, but not for the JMT thru-hikers. The JMT splits from the PCT before dramatically terminating high atop mighty Mount Whitney at 14,491 feet.

I looked forward to experiencing Sequoia National Park, which boasts the largest trees in the world. They're big enough to drive trucks through. They are trees that would make dinosaurs look like little house pets. We had been walking in sequoia tree country since the beginning of our trek but had not seen any at the elevations we were hiking.

Just days before Beth and I departed on our expedition, Sequoia National Park was plastered all over the news, not for the notably big trees but for the growing problem of Mexican drug cartels that harvested large marijuana crops in the national park. The hair-raising part of it was that in some cases they were operating within short distances of campers and hikers, and these guys meant business. They toted automatic assault rifles, undeterred by law enforcement and park rangers. I didn't want to alarm Beth with this information and give her one more thing to worry about. Besides, we weren't wearing DEA or law enforcement memorabilia, and I figured that these marijuana farmers would have at least enough sense to avoid the popular John Muir Trail area. At least, I hoped so. Part of me still secretly worried about what to do should we encounter any of these pot growers. I knew only enough Spanish to order margaritas and burritos politely in a Mexican restaurant with the help of a menu, so there would probably be a huge communication barrier.

The sun set rapidly as Beth and I descended Forester Pass. Reality set in that we would still be walking after dark, so we put on our headlamps during one of our brief rests. We didn't really need our headlamps, though, with the full moon guiding our way from a star-filled, cloudless sky. The trail

grade became more subtle, and we soon walked along a relatively flat, treeless, rocky area and passed Kiley's and Rick's
camp a short distance off the trail. We waved and continued
to walk, not wanting to interrupt their solitude. The moon
shimmered off distant lakes, and bear-sized boulders glowed
in the moonlight like kryptonite. The howl of coyotes inter-
rupted the still and silent night, scaring Beth, but to me it
was soothing. I cautiously kept an eye out for any machine-
gun-toting marijuana farmers and decided that surrender
would be our only recourse if we encountered those outlaws.
Beth stumbled quite a bit, partly because she has a difficult
time seeing at night and partly due to exhaustion. Tired and
hungry, we reached a trail junction in a scattered tree-covered
canopy within earshot of the white noise of a stream. This
was as far as we were going to walk. We assembled our tent,
boiled water for dinner, and finally snuggled into our sleeping bags. We had walked 23 miles over two mountain passes.
Only one more mountain pass remained, and so far no pot
growers or sequoia trees.

Chapter 21
The Mighty Whitney

The Summit of Mount Whitney, 211 miles from Happy Isles
August 13, 2003

Some accomplishments leave you speechless. Completing a long-distance trek across very rugged terrain is one of them. For that reason, there is no better way to end a long walk than to summit the mightiest mountain in the contiguous United States. The John Muir Trail visionaries did it right by ending the trail at Mount Whitney, elevation 14,491 feet. When words can't say it, mountains can. My Appalachian Trail expedition ended high atop Mount Katahdin. At 5,267 feet, it's a mild elevation in comparison to Whitney, but after hand-over-hand climbing, its mile-high views were a dramatic finish to a life-altering journey. It cemented my expectations of how a long-distance hike should end. The John Muir Trail wasn't about to disappoint. We hadn't really processed the fact that we were near the end of our journey. Even though we were only two days away from the end of the trail, we simply had been taking our journey one day at a time—the way life used to be.

It was August 12, and we were a little more than 20 miles from Mount Whitney. We planned to finish the next day by descending the other side to the Whitney Portal and rendez-vousing with Beth's parents and Aunt Pat. This day, we would walk just 13 miles, and we would do it slowly. Our food supply was running low, so were rationing more precisely than we had in the past.

Morning arrived quickly. We both were tired and could have slept into the afternoon, but our tent rapidly was becoming a sauna as the sun climbed high into the morning sky. Our muscles were sore after walking 23 miles over two mountain passes into the night. As we sat sipping our morning coffee, brightly colored tents caught our attention. We had been so focused on the trail and setting up camp the night before that we didn't even notice other campers.

Low-flying fighter jets from a nearby military facility shat-tered the silence from the calm blue sky. They zipped over the mountains and whizzed overhead, their screaming engines interrupting the natural hum of the wilderness. We began to encounter increasing numbers of hikers, numbers we hadn't seen since hiking away from Yosemite National Park weeks ago. Most of the hikers we saw weren't walking the JMT; they were backpacking a smaller loop. As a rule of thumb, an increase in people usually indicates that you are close to civilization, tourist attractions, and parking lots.

We trudged like worn-out packhorses. Our goal was to reach Guitar Lake on the west side of Mount Whitney. It would leave only a short distance to the summit in the morning with an eight-and-a-half-mile descent to Whitney Portal. We strolled in and out of shade most of the day and forded occasional small tributaries. We didn't have any major passes to cross until the next day, and the trail offered only small ups and downs. Beth stopped in a grassy field sprinkled with yellow wildflowers like a child who didn't want to take another step. She kind of fell and sat down in the same motion, and she insisted that I do the same, pulling me down by my arm. We both looked for excuses to take breaks all morning. Because we were low on food, we took more breaks to make up for our lack of energy.

We passed the final junction where the Pacific Crest Trail splits from the John Muir Trail. The JMT turns hard east toward Mount Whitney, while the PCT continues southward toward Mexico. A short walk from there, we stopped in a tree-shaded, grassy area known as Crabtree Meadow and took a long nap under a tree. We had only a few miles to Guitar Lake over treeless, sun-exposed terrain, so we decided to wait out the heat of the day in the shade. Later, we spotted an inviting ranger outpost cabin surrounded by large trees. The ranger lived in this rustic cabin during the busy season, so we paid him a visit and talked about the trail and our journey. He was married to another ranger posted near where we had camped the night before. The ranger seemed upbeat about his duties and wished us the best on the completion of our journey. We set out toward Guitar Lake.

We followed Whitney Creek through a shaded conifer forest and eventually left the tree canopy. We skirted a small lake, stopping occasionally to gawk at the mighty Mount Whitney, which now towered over us like the king of mountains. We continued climbing above the trees until we reached Guitar Lake, a small body of water that was wide at one end with half circle humps on opposite banks and narrow at the other end, giving the illusion of an acoustic guitar.

We walked past a group of men sitting around their campsite. Dozens of tents speckled the barren area all around. We found a flat tent pad along the lakeshore in the shadow of Mount Whitney. Rocks were piled knee-high in a small, shed-size square that marked the perimeter of our camp. We dropped our packs and went to work assembling our mountain abode for our last night. It was hard to believe that this was the last night that we would spend on the trail. Logistically, it was time to finish our journey as we were almost completely out of food. All day, we split candy bars and energy bars in half instead of our usual one-for-you, one-for-me mode of snacking. We had one freeze-dried dinner left—an unappealing lime chicken rice—one foil-wrapped package of ready-to-eat chicken, two energy bars, and one candy bar. Beth and I could easily eat all of this in one sitting, but we had to spread it out through the next afternoon to get us up and over Mount Whitney and down to Whitney Portal, about 15 miles. I hoped I could catch some fish to supplement our waning food supplies.

Beth relaxed against a large rock while I stood along the lakeshore and cast my fish line into the water. First one bite, then another, and finally I hooked one and reeled it in. It wasn't much bigger than a sardine, so I threw it back and continued casting. I caught several miniature trout that were too small to bother with. Beth was growing impatient with hunger.

"Jeff, do you want to give up with the fishing and just eat what we have?" she asked irritably. The freeze-dried meals claim to serve two, but I think the makers based the serving size on children as opposed to hungry hikers. Beth and I easily could consume one freeze-dried entrée each and still have room for more. I didn't want to go to bed hungry, especially knowing there were fish in the lake.

"Let me fish a while longer," I hollered. A short time later, there was a tug at my line. I slowly reeled it in. A trout about eight inches long dangled off my hook as I carefully reeled it to shore. God must have placed this trout on my line, I thought.

"Beth, this is our Mount Whitney protein ... a gift from God," I said, big eyed and drooling, as I pulled the fish off the hook and went to work cleaning it with my Swiss Army knife. Within a few minutes, our trout was submerged in boiling butter water. We devoured the trout as soon as it was cooked and then choked down the lime chicken dinner. After dinner, we were left with two energy bars, a foil pouch of chicken, and a candy bar to split between us. We left it unsaid that we would be starving by midday the next day. I tried to put those thoughts aside.

I thought we had seen the best of the Sierra sunsets and sunrises, but Mother Nature had a few more to share. As the sun set that evening, Mount Whitney turned an almond-tinged white, and the sky above the mountain took on a midnight blue shade as we stood speechless, snapping pictures. The next morning around 6 a.m., we climbed out of our tent into the brisk, 40-degree morning to witness the most extraordinary sunrise we had ever seen. The emerging sun illuminated distant mountains with brilliant shades of orange, while the full moon persisted, hanging luminous in the blue sky. Our tent door overlooked the calm, mirror-like lake, and we still were submerged in the shadow of a mountain on the opposite shoreline. I captured this moment on film, and later

I wrote this poem:

Morning's Reflection:
A sunrise that slowly illuminates the beginning of a new day
the moon still present as a reminder of a peaceful night
darkness slowly fading, allowing a gradual acceptance
of the new light
A lake without a ripple, a calm reflection of the beauty
that surrounds
A new day has sprung with God's glory all around.

We weren't out of the woods yet. We had to go up and over Mount Whitney, the highest elevation of our journey. We had been blessed with great weather ever since the first few days of rain ended. But we knew the weather could change on a dime, raising the rivers with rain or even snow, and because we would be so far above tree line, we would be exposed continually to the possibility of lightning. Then there was hypothermia. A 1979 *Washington Post Magazine* article chronicled the adventures of a woman who walked the John Muir Trail. On her climb over Mount Whitney, she encountered rain, snow, and high rivers. She witnessed the hypothermic death of two hikers, and a total of five people died on the climb.

Beth and I sipped our morning coffee and decided to split the foil-wrapped chicken for breakfast, saving our two energy bars and one candy bar for the climb. We broke camp and began our ascent around 7:30. We were refreshed from a light day of walking yesterday, a good night's rest, and thoughts of reaching more food at the end. The trail was a sidewalk-wide shelf hanging off the steep side of the mountain as it zigzagged its way to the top. We came upon a man standing along the trail shortly after we left camp. He stood off to the side of the trail, keeled over and pale as if he would vomit at any moment. He said he felt nauseated and wasn't used to the altitude. He was waiting for his group to catch up and said he would be fine, so we left him and kept walking. We could see a hiker moving rather slowly a few cliff-edge shelves above us. The distance narrowed between the struggling hiker and us, and we soon caught up. The hiker was a woman with long, gray hair who wore a vintage 1970s external-frame backpack. Her face was painted by hard, painful life. Leathery wrinkles were etched around her eyes, nose, and mouth like the rings of a tree. She was carrying a bucket-size bear canister on one hand and a walking stick in the other. The woman was working her way to the top slowly along the narrow cliff-edge trail. She would take five small, shuffling steps and stop for a period longer than it took to take the steps. Watching her was painful. We were afraid she would collapse any minute.

"Excuse me, ma'am, can I carry your food bucket to the top for you?" I asked.

"No," she replied. "I'm just fine."

"It's really no problem. My pack is nearly empty," I persisted.

"Thank you, but I'm fine."

"Are you hiking with anyone?"

"What you see is what you get."

"Well, take care of yourself," I offered as Beth and I passed her. We were worried for her out there all alone in such a feeble state. She looked like she was in pain, but what more could we do? If she were a relative of mine, I would have insisted on taking her equipment from her and helping her off the mountain.

We ran into pockets of hikers all morning as we climbed up the west side of Mount Whitney. As we neared the top, we would encounter gobs more. Most of the nearly 20,000 hikers who summit Mount Whitney each year hike up from Whitney Portal on the eastern side. After a few hours of thin-air hiking, Beth and I came to the trail crest where the east and west trails met. From there, we could continue down the east side or choose a side trail along the ridge. The side trail was an additional four-mile round trip to the actual summit, and we planned to hike it. Most backpackers leave their heavy loads at the trail crest and downsize to a daypack to increase their agility. Already, a dozen or more packs were lined up at the crest. Tourists were milling all about, many looking nauseated and pale, some leaning over the side of the trail to vomit. They obviously ignored the recommendations to acclimate before climbing to such an elevation. It is estimated that as many as 500 people a day walk up Mount Whitney in season.

Beth and I dropped our packs with the others and removed the top pouch from Beth's pack. We packed some water and the last of our food to carry with us. We took my Therm-a-Rest mattress pad, which we were going to use for photos at the summit. The night before, we tore strips of duct tape and taped them to the mattress pad to spell out: HIKE FOR MIKE JMT 218 MILES. We turned to begin our final climb and stopped to read a newspaper-size metal sign: "Extreme danger from lightning. To avoid being struck by lightning, immediately leave the area if any of the following conditions exist: dark clouds nearby, thunder, hail, or rain, hissing in the air, static electricity in the hair or fingertips. The Whitney shelter will not offer protection. You should leave the summit and proceed to a lower elevation." The metal roof of the shelter actually conducts electricity, and hikers have been killed inside the shelter. I wondered why the shelter was built if it wouldn't actually offer shelter.

Along the narrow cliff-edge walk, we encountered Kiley and Rick on their way back down from the summit. Apparently, they passed us while we took a break at Crabtree Meadow the day before and had camped high above Guitar Lake with a bird's-eye view of all of us camped along the lakeshore. We snapped their picture, congratulated them on their accomplishment, and moved along. We continued walking along the west side of the ridge and could see Guitar Lake down in the valley. Its shape certainly did resemble that of an acoustic guitar. We passed tourists all along the two-mile route to the top.

Sixteen days after we left Curry Village in Yosemite National Park, we summited Mount Whitney. We knew we were at the summit when the shelter house came into view. We trotted the final hundred yards until we reached the hut. Beth signed our names into the official register that was kept in a metal box with a hinged lid. Just past the shelter, a truck-size boulder with a tablet bolted to it announced: "Mt. Whitney Elevation 14,496.811 Ft., John Muir Trail – High Sierra Trail, September 5, 1930." It went on to say: "This tablet marks the construction of the highest trail in the United States. ..." We unfolded our sign and asked a nearby tourist to take our picture as we held it up across the Mount Whitney sign. Beth and I embraced each other. Tears trickled from Beth's eyes. We had done it. It was a happy moment after a long, hard, journey in honor of a good man.

Hundreds of people were walking around the relatively

flat, rocky summit. Several folks asked about our hike in accents from all over the world. As Beth explained our cause, the responses were overwhelming. Tourists congratulated us. Several mentioned friends and relatives who suffered from depression. It was clear that ours was a global issue.

We sat along the eastern edge, looking down into the valley. We had a clear view of Lone Pine, the town where we planned to meet Beth's parents later that day. The sound of metal clanking below our feet startled us. Two climbers appeared at our feet as they scaled the final few feet up the eastern face and pulled themselves up from the cliff side. They were wearing climbing helmets, and carabiners dangled off their chests like military medals. They had climbed nearly 2,000 feet straight up a sheer rock face. I guess they preferred a more challenging journey to the top than we had chosen.

A pile of rocks off to the side of the shelter served as a barrier to the pit toilet just beyond it. As soon as Beth saw the toilet, she was determined to use it. I guess it symbolized domesticated amenities to her, although it was little more than a hole dynamited into the rock with a toilet seat placed over it. While Beth relieved herself on the highest toilet in the country, I shooed away a group of Boy Scouts trying to get a glimpse of the mysterious female anatomy.

We ate our energy bars and began our 11-mile descent, which went much more quickly than our climb. We picked up our packs at the trail crest and rounded a bend in the trail that brought us around to the east side of the mountain. Just then we spotted the elderly woman a few shelves below us, shuffling along at the same struggling pace as earlier. We quickly caught up to her again.

"Please, let me carry your food bucket. I promise I won't

eat any of it," I pleaded.

The woman remembered us from earlier and sat down on a rock. She clenched her teeth in pain as she rested. Then she said, "Look, I appreciate your offers to help me, but I'm fine. My father had several problems when he died—lung cancer, emphysema, and diabetes, to name a few. My lungs really hurt, and I'm sure that I have a few of my father's illnesses, but I will get over this mountain. I've got all day."

Beth and I stood mesmerized in awe at her strength to push along despite obvious pain and suffering. I told her to take care of herself, and Beth and I walked on. Talk about perseverance, mind over body, or ignorance—I'm still not sure which, but she was doing it. The woman shouted to us as we descended: "After this trip, I think I'll stick to car camping."

Beth and I walked for miles, dramatically dropping in elevation down the switchbacks. We came to Trail Camp at 12,000 feet, where many of the Mount Whitney climbers stay to acclimate before making the final climb. I pulled out our last piece of food—a melted Snickers bar—tore it open, and broke it in half for us to share. We were officially foodless on the trail. We stood up and continued walking when a man's voice shouted, "Wait!" We turned around in the direction of the voice. A park ranger sat on a rock shaded by the wall of a nearby bathroom facility with his black Labrador retriever.

"Can I see your permits?" he asked.

"No one has asked us for our permits the entire journey," I told him as I took off my pack and fumbled through my top compartment in search of our permit. I handed the ranger the piece of paper authorizing our passage. As he scanned it, I wondered what would happen if our permit was invalid. Would we be sent back the way we came? The ranger returned our permit and congratulated us on our journey. I pulled out my camera and asked if we could commemorate him as the first and only official to check our hiking credentials. He obliged. We continued along, dropping below tree line as we zigzagged down the mountain.

Beth's parents, Kathy and Larry, were helping out with our adventure every way they could. Our hike had given them something tangible to concentrate on in the fog of grief over their lost son. We had made plans to meet them at Whitney Portal, a campground outpost at the bottom of the trail we were descending. Before our journey, they had helped sell Hike For Mike T-shirts at the Chicago Board of Trade. Using their frequent-flyer miles, they had bought us our round-trip airfare to the Sierra, and now they had flown in from Chicago, along with Beth's Aunt Pat from Seattle, to meet us. It meant a lot to Beth to have her parents and aunt meet us at the end. It rekindled the warm feelings I had when my family met me at the end of my Appalachian Trail adventure. Because we couldn't pinpoint our exact day and time of finish until recently, they had arrived days earlier and were touring the area as we coordinated with them by satellite phone.

We heard from other hikers that the camp store made excellent cheeseburgers and sold cold beer. That's all I could think about for the last few miles down the mountain. The trail had become a long, arduous line to the food counter. My pace picked up the more I thought about food. Beth understood without a word and picked her pace up as well. Her thought process had become as one-track as mine. As we whizzed by other hikers, I would shout, "Passing on your left!

Cheeseburgers at the bottom." We were getting some strange looks, so Beth would shout back, "We haven't had real food in days!"

We came across a sign announcing the end of John Muir Wilderness. We began to see the campers and tents that had been camouflaged below the canopy of pine trees. We had reached Whitney Portal. The trail spit out into a parking lot near some picnic benches and bathrooms. Beth immediately saw her mom and aunt standing near a picnic bench.

"Mom!" Beth shouted.

Beth's mom and Aunt Pat hurried over and embraced us, with no regard to our warnings of how bad we smelled. Beth's mom handed Beth six long-stemmed yellow roses. Everyone was holding back tears.

"Where is Larry?" I asked.

Before anyone had a chance to reply, the spring-loaded outhouse door swung open, and Larry walked out.

"Hey! Hey, guys!" he shouted, walking toward us with a newspaper tucked under his arm. He handed it to me and said, "I got this for you."

I was so curious about what was going in the world that I gladly took the tainted newspaper. Did they find Saddam yet? Is Arnold Schwarzenegger the governor of California? Can you still buy cheeseburgers? Because Beth's parents and aunt couldn't be with us atop Mount Whitney, we pulled out our "Hike For Mike" mattress sign, and we all held it across our fronts for a picture, the symbolic end to our journey.

Chapter 22
Moving On:
One Step at a Time

Whitney Portal, 221 miles from Happy Isles
August 13, 2003

Beth and I fully understood why the California bears are drawn to heavily populated tourist areas. Our olfactory senses were teased by a smell we knew all too well: burgers charring on the grill. We made our way to the camp store and ordered up the cheeseburgers and fries we had salivated about for the past several days. The glow of a significant accomplishment was temporarily suppressed by one of life's basic needs. This was only the beginning of our food binge. We then climbed into Beth's parents' rental car. We really needed showers, and Beth's dad immediately powered down all the windows as we drove further down the mountain to Lone Pine to check into motel rooms and prepare for an even bigger meal. Lone Pine sits between Death Valley and Mount Whitney in close proximity to Hollywood. Film production crews have used the mountain views as backdrops in many movies with legendary actors such as John Wayne and Clint

Eastwood. More recent films shot there include *Gladiator* and *G.I. Jane.*

Having been without domestic amenities for the last 16 days, Beth and I felt like aliens in our hotel room. Flushing toilets, washing our hands in the sink, and flicking through channels on the TV were a dramatic contrast to our lifestyle on the trail. We thought for sure the shower drain would clog from the silt running off our bodies. After cycling through our showers, we stood staring at the drain as it slowly absorbed the foul water, making desperate sucking noises as the water disappeared and left a gritty residue across the tub basin.

We called our webmaster, Georgia, and gave her our last update to post on the website. We told her about our Mount Whitney climb and how we made a "Hike For Mike" sign that we held up when we reached the summit. We detailed how we found Beth's mom, dad, and aunt at the base of the mountain and that we were heading out for a big meal to celebrate. Georgia posted our last update promptly on our website for everyone to know that we'd made it.

We met Beth's parents and aunt outside our room and drove to a nearby steak house that Beth's dad had scouted out earlier. Beth's mom, dad, and aunt were eager to hear about our adventures, but Beth and I were more focused on the food. Beth wolfed down an entire slab of ribs and a loaf of chocolate mousse cake with ice cream, and I gnawed down a 16-ounce rib eye steak, potatoes, salad, and a few beers—Sierra Nevada Pale Ale, of course.

The next day, we drove to Sequoia National Forest to see the most massive plants on the face of the earth. We stood inside one tree, which easily accommodated all of us with room left for a few cars. Then Beth's dad and I walked up to a tree to pose for a photo as we tried to wrap our arms around the trunk. Our arm spans barely stretched beyond one root. We were so small in comparison to these mammoth trees that they reminded me that we exist in a world created by a being much greater than us. Our creator has the capability of creating plant life of such enormous size that he surely must be capable of fathoming ideas we can't possibly comprehend. These enormous trees made me feel helpless and simple, much the same as Beth, our family, and everyone who knew Mike felt when we learned of his death. What I have learned is that it's okay to feel helpless at times. That's part of being human.

Our John Muir Trail adventure was only a tenth of the distance I walked during my five-month expedition on the Appalachian Trail. But in many ways, Beth and I walked beyond my Appalachian Trail expedition in ways you can't measure with a pedometer. Our relationship developed in ways we never thought. Our depression awareness campaign seemed to have a ripple effect, and I hoped our adventure helped my grieving wife and her family in a small way as they continued to work through such a tragic loss.

Beth and I were more than husband and wife during our adventure. We were a team. We had to be. Even four years of marriage didn't prepare us for the tedious issues of walking together along some of the most rugged and remote terrain in the country. Adjusting to each other's cadence was difficult. Everyone has his or her own pace, much as in reading books, eating, and most everything we do in life. Walking in step with each other for nearly three weeks brought us together and taught us to be more mindful of each other's strengths and weaknesses. We took turns being the engine and the caboose, pulling and pushing each other along as we tackled the Sierra. Hiking with my wife has expanded our relationship into new areas. Although every day was difficult, a wild Tarzan-Jane romantic flare evolved on the trail from sitting together before phenomenal alpenglow sunsets, walking along in view of breathless mountain vistas, and camping along refreshing, serene glacial lakes.

My wife is my hero. She managed to keep her positive demeanor even when she felt disgusting and wore only two outfits without a shower for days on end, when she suffered a bruised knee and torn pants from a dangerous fall, and as she endured agonizing blisters and gnawing hunger. I knew she had crossed over to hiker woman when in spite of her discomfort in water and hatred of being cold, she plunged herself into a glacial lake just to get rid of the stink. As we chatted with Beth's parents and aunt over dinner, I looked at and listened to my wife with newfound admiration for her strength and courage to do this difficult walk. Beth now could add thru-hiker to her athletic resume. She was motivated to walk the trail partly to work through the loss of her brother, partly to bring awareness about depression to others, and partly to be with her husband doing what he loves. In the process of healing, Beth had managed to celebrate successes along the way.

Our journey was spiritual. It offered many deeper meanings that we have only begun to comprehend. We remember leaving some key provisions back in Yosemite, and just when we were considering backtracking down the mountain, a hiker appeared around the bend and had the answer to our dilemma. We learned we could help each other during life's crises. We also look back on encountering the boy perched on a rock, fearing for his life as a bear circled him and wanting only his dad. The boy's dad was his hero much the same as Mike was to his son, wife, stepdaughter, parents, siblings, and friends. We all have an inner hero, whether we realize it or not. Unfortunately, Mike didn't recognize what a hero he was. Then there was the elderly woman we encountered on Mount Whitney. The woman was obviously in pain, but although her situation was less than ideal, she remained focused on her goal and went after it. "I've got all day," she said. By focusing on our goals and dreams, we can get through life's hardships one step at a time.

John Muir got it right when he wrote, "Thousands of tired, nerve shaken, over civilized people are beginning to find out that going to the mountains is going home; that wilderness is a necessity, and that mountain parks and reservations are useful not only as fountains of timber and irrigating rivers, but as fountains of life." There is no better way to honor this most influential naturalist, credited with inspiring the creation of America's national parks, than by dedicating a beautiful trail in his honor. The John Muir Trail was the perfect venue for Beth and me to advocate for depression awareness. A plaque in one of our national parks quotes Muir: "Everyone needs beauty as well as bread, places to play, where nature may heal and cheer and give strength to body and soul." Muir knew the physical and mental benefits of escaping into the backcountry long before most others did. Today, most physicians agree that walking and hiking in the great outdoors not only helps with the physical well-being but also rejuvenates the mind, relieving stress and aiding in the treatment of depression.

Our goal of the "Hike For Mike" awareness campaign was

to offer hope and a breath of positive energy during a difficult time. We can't change the past, but we hope we can help prevent a similar tragedy from happening to someone else. We received hundreds of heartfelt e-mails, cards, and letters in support of our walk, and we responded to all of them. Hundreds sympathized with our cause; some expressed personal struggles with depression or that of a friend or loved one, and some shared sad and unfortunate stories of someone that had committed suicide. We had helped draw attention to this treatable mental disorder.

Beth and I returned safely, filled with miles of new life. We had walked along for 218 miles over the course of 16 days, burning at least 5,000 calories a day, giving our cardio systems an intense workout with the thin air and continuous motion. We removed layers of stress and worry by putting aside our hectic schedules and focusing purely on walking, eating, sleeping, and more walking. We lived a simple life and concentrated on our core selves. We were so inspired by our journey that when we returned home, we dedicated a room in our house to the Sierra by painting the walls as blue as the Sierra sky and posting John Muir quotes alongside some of our spectacular photos. We have reflected back on our John Muir Trail adventure on many occasions. Beth has a new-found confidence and is willing to go after new challenges like never before. I know one thing for sure: I not only have a wife who is beautiful both inside and out, I have a hiking partner on the path of life.

Our journey was incredible. The first few days of our hike, we encountered gray skies, rain, and the adversity of leaving behind some vital gear. But we retrieved the gear with the help of others; the weather cleared up; and we bore witness to some of the bluest sky and absorbing sun of our entire journey. In some ways, it symbolized depression. Many with clinical depression see only gray skies, but by forging ahead, getting help from a physician, taking the right medication or therapy, and embarking on a walking or exercise routine, people suffering from depression can summit the mountain from the dark valley of depression and see the all blue sky that this world offers. A successful journey begins by taking those first steps and overcoming each mountain one step at a time.

Each spring, Mother Nature brings fresh life into the world with brilliant flowers, leaves, and warmth, and each fall brings the awe-inspiring change of colors. On September 22, 2004, the fall equinox, Mother Nature marked not only a change in season but also a new adventure in our life with the birth of a baby girl, Madison. To keep the wanderlust alive, we have discussed ideas of where our first family hike with our daughter will be: a walk across Ireland, a trek in Australia, perhaps an excursion from hut to hut in the Swiss Alps, or the mountains of Hawaii, or a walk across America, a return trip to the John Muir Trail, or maybe another Appalachian Trail hike. Of course, we most likely will stick to shorter journeys until Madison can carry her own supplies. One thing is for sure: we are going to walk together along the path of life and help each other climb every one of life's mountains while supporting each other through the valleys. As a family, we will continue to set the biggest of goals and go after them one step at a time.

From Beth's Side
of the Tent

Written by Beth Alt

I never dreamed I could hike more than 200 miles with a 30-plus pound pack on my back. I didn't really want to, either. I always admired my husband for the energy and drive he showed by completing a 2,000-plus mile hike, but I never felt the same desire to step out of the box of life and carry my life on my back for an extended period of time. When I was younger, my family went on outings in our pop-up camper, but it wasn't something that interested me as an adult. After all, a hot shower did wonders after a great workout, and that would not be an option on the trail. My outlook shifted, however, when I lost my big brother Mike to suicide in 2002. Everything changed in an instant. Mike's death crumbled our hopes and shattered our dreams. It was the unthinkable. I went through all of the denial and blame, and sometimes I still wonder if there was something I could have done to save him.

Mike was a great guy. He wasn't perfect—none of us is—but he was a genuine, caring, loving man. I looked up to him. I was the maid of honor at his wedding. I helped him move several times, and he helped me move to Cincinnati after I decided to go back to school. He set up my stereo and computer in minutes when it would have taken me hours. He had a lot of gifts, especially the ability to make other people smile. Unfortunately, he was not smiling on the inside, and we didn't know that until after he was gone. You don't know how good you have it until tragedy strikes. Mike was supposed to grow old with me and be an uncle to my kids. He was meant to be an awesome father. His life seemed great, but it was not perfect. Mike was suffering from depression. He did not know it, or, if he did, he did not know what to do about it.

I am a speech language pathologist. In my job, I teach kids to communicate better. Ironically, the missing link in death by suicide turned out to be communication. I never knew the weight of despair my brother carried on his back. Suddenly, the idea of taking a long hike with a heavy pack on my back seemed attainable, even appropriate. I saw some pictures of the John Muir Trail from Jeff's hiking buddy, and afterward, I decided that I wanted to hike for Mike. It was too late to help my brother, but I knew that many other people might be contemplating actions like Mike's. I wanted to help them. So Jeff and I decided to do an awareness campaign for depression to link what now is obvious to me: depression can lead to suicide. I never really put the two together, but I found out that the majority of suicides happen because of untreated depression. Awareness is the first step in prevention, so my husband, the avid hiker, and I, the novice, decided to embark on a journey to increase depression awareness.

I did the unthinkable. I went for weeks without a shower. I relieved myself outdoors, came within a few feet of a bear, and slept in a tent night after night. It definitely was an out-of-the-box experience for me, but sharing it with my husband was both healing and inspiring. The journey made me appreciate my husband, my physical endurance, the beauty of nature, and my family all the more. In the end, we accomplished what we set out to do. We finished the hike and took our message across the country through the media. I know Mike would be proud of me, and maybe he was smiling down from heaven when we met my mom and dad and aunt at the end of our journey.

Thanks to all of our family and friends who supported us on this journey; to our gear and financial sponsors; to those who purchased T-shirts and allowed us to donate a large sum of money to the Suicide Prevention Action Network USA; to the media that wrote and ran stories that helped our awareness goal; to our webmaster, who helped us to keep everyone abreast of our journey; and to everyone who prayed for our safe journey. With this team of helpers, we were able to raise awareness of depression. We received many e-mails, some thanking us for what we were doing for depression and suicide prevention, some that shared personal or family battles with depression. We were touched by many. We feel that we made a difference, but it's not enough. We can do more.

In this country, someone dies by suicide every 17 minutes. Every 17 minutes. And yet people continue to joke about "jumping off a bridge" or saying they'll "kill themselves" if this or that happens, like it means nothing. Since I lost my brother to suicide, I find that kind of thing terribly unfunny. People aren't trying to be mean or insensitive, but this is no joking matter. Also, "suicide" is the bad word here, not "depression." It's time to shed the stigma that's attached to depression. It is not a character flaw. It is not a condition to be ashamed of or a fate to blame on your family. It is a chemical imbalance. It can be diagnosed medically. And if it's left untreated, it can lead to death. We must bring down the walls and end the shame and the stigma that are attached to depression and start treating it like the illness that it is.

Our journey was one of hope. We hope to prevent suicides, and we want to instill hope in those with depression, so that they know that treatments exist and that one does not have to face the demons of depression alone. When we reached the top of Mount Whitney, I felt a sadness, but also a rush of satisfaction, joy, and exuberance. Energy and good feelings come from exercise and fresh air. Many people with depression can benefit from daily exercise and light therapy, in addition to prescribed medication, counseling, group therapy, and other treatments. My best thoughts happen during a run, a walk, a hike, or a spinning class. My husband's best thoughts occur during a hike. Maybe that's because we force away all the weight and stress in our daily lives. It allows us to refocus on what's important.

It comes down to this: you don't have to be perfect. Just do the best that you can. That's a mantra that my sister-in-law shared with me when I asked how she did it all, how she managed to be a good mom, a good wife, a good employee, everything. She said, "Just do the best you can, and you may need to redefine your definition of 'good.'" That is so simple, but so profound. My husband says, "Life is as simple or complicated as you make it." Do we make life too complicated by trying to juggle everything and not just sitting back and enjoying the ride? Maybe people with depression don't know that they don't have to be perfect, that there is hope, that if they just hold onto their loved ones, there can be light at the end of the tunnel. We don't know how long we are on this Earth, so we have to live life wholeheartedly. We need to live in the moment, relax, enjoy family and friends, and tell them how much they mean to us. We can't say it enough. If nothing else, I know that the last time I spoke with Mike, I told him that I loved him. At least I have that.

Besides lugging a heavy backpack down a very long trail, I've done something else I didn't think was possible: I became a mom. We have been blessed with two wonderful children, Madison and William. They have added so much joy to our lives. I know Mike would have loved to spending time with them. I know he is smiling down on our families. I am grateful to my husband for being a great father to our children, but also for giving me the strength and confidence to do what I thought impossible: to hike for Mike.

Afterword

11 Years Later with Jeff Alt

It has been eleven years since our expedition along the John Muir Trail. The adventurous bond formed between Beth and me remains strong. Our JMT journey was just what we needed at that point in our life. Beth experienced what I already knew, that there are healing powers that come from a walk in the woods and mountains. Beth continues to enjoy hiking and eagerly joins me on new adventures.

Four Boots One Journey was originally published in 2005 as *A Hike for Mike* and we launched it from the steps of the U.S. Capitol. In September 2005, two years after our expedition, our hike took a metaphorical twist. Event planners in Washington D.C. who had followed our John Muir Trail adventure, invited us to lead a walk to Capitol Hill dubbed "Hike to the Hill." This was a suicide prevention/depression awareness rally organized by a national coalition of mental health agencies. I'm not one to jump into the political arena, but legislation for mental health awareness had recently cleared congress, with overwhelming bipartisan support, and was signed into law by the president of the United States.

On the day of our original book release, Beth, our young daughter, Beth's parents, and a few extended relatives joined me in leading the "Hike to the Hill." Beth's parents carried the "Hike to the Hill" banner. We were followed by hundreds of supporters, many of them advocating for a friend or loved one. When we reached the U.S Capitol, I was honored to share the speaking podium with U.S. Senator Gordon Smith (R-OR), his wife Sharon, and Dianna Baitinger, Miss Connecticut 2005. Senator Gordon Smith was the architect of the recent mental health legislation signed into law by the president, the Garrett Lee Smith Memorial Act. Miss Connecticut, a talented singer, sang "America the Beautiful." The American flag flew above the U.S. Capitol and fluttered majestically in the wind as we all stood listening to Dianna sing the lyrics of our nation's song. This event was physically a far cry from our grueling hike across the Sierra's via the John Muir Trail. We were without the high mountain thin air, blistered feet, hunger, and sweat. But, we were on the steps of the U.S. Capitol and symbolically passing legislation can be a far more intellectual grueling climb than physically hiking the John Muir Trail. A feeling of pride and accomplishment set in as we stood with a U.S. senator, a Miss USA contestant, and hundreds of others who had succeeded in passing legislation for mental health awareness. Sometimes tragedy results in positive change. It was a family crisis that had brought about our John Muir Trail hike. What makes this country so great is that we have the freedom to come to together and unite around a common cause and make a positive change.

The pomp and circumstance of all the events surrounding our hike on the trail and the capitol steps have faded, but remain burned in our memory and shared in this book. Beth still misses her brother but she feels proud that she completed our "Hike for Mike" in hopes of preventing a tragedy in another family. Beth still has moments of sadness when thinking about her brother, but she's found that by putting a smile on her face and remembering the positive moments she had with him, she is able move forward.

Our family has grown in amazing ways. We now have two children, Madison and William. We've been keeping busy trying to be the best parents we can. They have added so much joy to our lives and they are growing up fast.

The annual Sunshine Walk inspired from my Appalachian Trail journey and chronicled in my book, *A Walk for Sunshine,* continues. As I write this, we are preparing for the 17th annual event. Sunshine supports over 1,000 individuals with developmental disabilities, including my brother Aaron. Aaron was born with cerebral palsy. He is intellectually impaired, non-verbal, and unable to walk or control his motor movements. Yet, he always has a contagious smile. I dedicated my Appalachian Trail journey to Aaron and walked the Appalachian Trail as a fundraiser for Sunshine. It's hard to believe that 17 years ago, seventy-five people turned out for the first Walk With Sunshine, symbolically in step with me, as I walked alone in the woods, over 2,000-miles along the Appalachian Trail. I may be the founder of the "Walk With Sunshine," but it was really my family, friends, Sunshine staff and residents, and the greater community that has made this event a success. Sunshine relies on donations and funds raised from this event to enhance the quality of life of those they serve. Our event has grown and evolved over the years. In 2013, over 800 participants turned out. To date, we've raised over $350,000. We've added a professionally timed 5k run and the event is now called the "Sunshine Walk, 5k Run & Roll." I continue to support and co-host the annual event accompanied by my wife, kids, parents, siblings, aunts, uncles, cousins and friends. Our kids have attended every Sunshine event since birth and they are growing up into compassionate and giving volunteers. Last year, my daughter sold rainbow loom bracelets and donated the money to Sunshine. Our kids have learned how special Sunshine is in caring for their Uncle Aaron and many others.

As parents, we realized the need to expose our kids to the outdoors at the youngest of ages. The great outdoors is a natural, multisensory place for kids to have fun and learn valuable lessons. TV, computer, and video game addictions are replacing outdoor play time. This passive inside entertainment is contributing significantly to the national obesity epidemic! We wanted to get out in front of this dilemma before our kids were ever exposed to anything that requires batteries or electricity. We wanted to show our kids how to have more fun outdoors than anything that requires electricity. We took both of our children on their first hikes before they were three months old. We trekked across a 50-mile path of Ireland carrying our 21-month old daughter, accompanied by extended family. Our son was on the Appalachian Trail at 8 weeks of age. Hiking as a family has become our routine and our kids love it.

As a hiking expert, having spent a lifetime on the trail, I realized that there are allot of families that craved advice on how to take their own kids hiking and make it fun. So, I began providing hiking with kids seminars in collaboration with the Shenandoah National Park Staff and other venues. I compiled all of my advice into a book, *Get Your Kids Hiking: How to Start Them Young and Keep it Fun,* which was released in 2013. My family and I have enjoyed traveling around sharing our hiking tips. We even have a song and dance we share called "Take a Hike."

We all need rejuvenation and a break from our routine. I've found that hiking is a holistic athletic endeavor that can be used as a tool to navigate through life. Hiking with family and friends is a natural time to really communicate and build your relationship while removed from the busy clutter of everyday life. Life is a journey and getting outdoors helps me to enjoy the present and celebrate the simple things that sometimes can only be found on a hike.

About the Author

Jeff Alt is a traveling speaker, hiking expert, and award-winning author of the popular Appalachian Trail book, *A Walk for Sunshine* and *Get Your Kids Hiking.* He presents inspiring and entertaining keynotes around the country and hiking seminars in and around National Parks. Alt has been hiking since his youth. He has walked the 2,160-mile Appalachian Trail, the 218-mile John Muir Trail with his wife, and he carried his 21-month old daughter on a family trek across Ireland. Alt has been hiking with his kids since they were infants. He is a member of the Outdoor Writers Association of America (OWAA). Alt lives with his wife and two children in Cincinnati, Ohio. For more information about Jeff Alt visit: www.jeffalt.com

Suggested Reading

- Beck, Steve. *Trout Fishing the John Muir Trail.* Portland, OR. Frank Amato Publications, 2000.
- Muir, John, Gleason, Herbert. *My First Summer in the Sierra.* New York, NY. Random House, 2003.
- Stetson, Lee, King, Fiona. *The Wild Muir.* Yosemite National Park, CA: Yosemite Association, 1994.
- Storer, Tracy. Usinger, Robert. Lukas, David. *Sierra Nevada Natural History.* Berkeley, CA. University of California Press, 2004.
- Robinson, Douglas. Starr, Walter. *Starr's Guide to the John Muir Trail and the High Sierra Region.* San Francisco, CA. Sierra Club Books, 1974.
- Winnett, Thomas. Morey, Kathy. *Guide To The John Muir Trail.* Berkeley, CA: Wilderness Press, 1998.

For more information on the John Muir Trail contact:

Pacific Crest Trail Association
1331 Garden Highway
Sacramento, CA 95833

916-285-1846
https://www.pcta.org/